D0410186

The Usborne
Book of
KnowHow

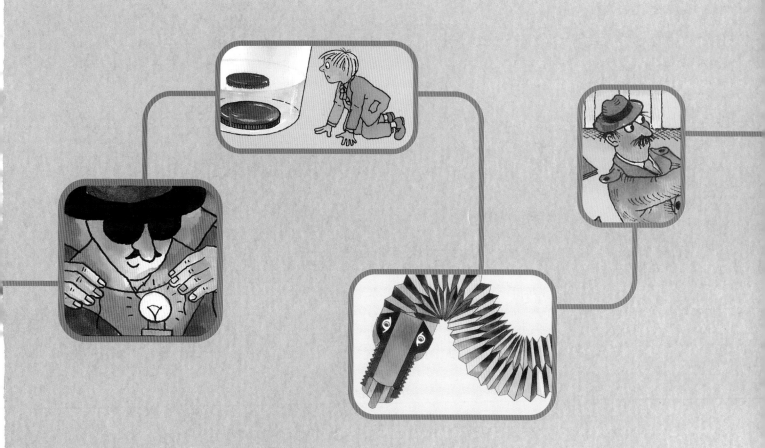

The Usborne Book of KnowHow

Heather Amery, Judy Hindley, Ian Adair,
Anne Civardi, Annabelle Curtis,
Donald Rumbelow and Falcon Travis

Illustrated by Colin King

Designed by John Jamieson,
Sally Burrough, Mike Olley and Zoe Wray

Edited by Kate Knighton

Contents

Spycraft

Carrying secret messages

One of the first spy tricks you should learn is how to deliver a secret message. Don't attract your enemy's attention by carrying a bag or holding suspicious-looking papers. With the Stick Scrambler shown below you can encode a message on a paper strip that is easy to hide. See the chart for the methods used by the Black Hat Spy for hiding messages.

Try removing the message with a quick and casual-looking movement – as though you are just hooking your thumb in your pocket or taking a pebble from your shoe. If you hide the message in a pen or hat you can pretend to leave it somewhere by accident, and then your spy can pick it up.

On the following pages you will find more details on where to hide your messages and how to pass them secretly to other spies. The answers to the codes in this section are on page 127.

Spy language:
A spy-friend is called a contact. A spy who carries messages is a courier. A spy who holds messages to be picked up is a 'letter-box'.

HIDING PLACES FOR MESSAGES

INSIDE HAT BAND

PINNED BEHIND LAPEL

BETWEEN STRAPS

INSIDE PEN

INSIDE CUFFS

SECRET POCKET BEHIND FLAP

INSIDE SOCK

UNDER FALSE SOLE OF SHOE

BLACK HAT SPY

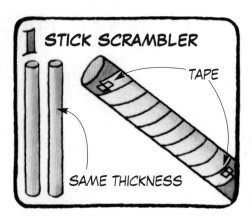

1 STICK SCRAMBLER

TAPE

SAME THICKNESS

Both you and your contact must have sticks of just the same thickness – try pencils. Wind a strip of paper tightly around your stick. Fasten it with sticky tape.

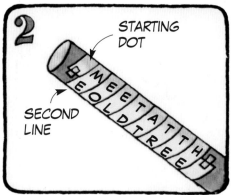

2

STARTING DOT

SECOND LINE

MEET AT THE OLD TREE

Write a message on the strip, like this. Make a dot beside the first letter to show your contact where the message starts. Turn the stick to add more lines.

3

Unwind the paper and the letters will be scrambled up. The message will be hidden until your contact winds the strip around a stick of exactly the same thickness.

1 FALSE SOLE

DRAW AROUND

Place your shoe on a piece of thin cardboard, such as a cereal box. Use a pencil to draw around it.

2

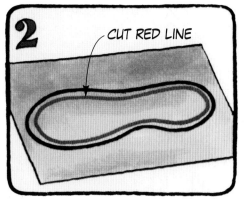

CUT RED LINE

Then, draw a line just inside the outline, like this. Cut this line to make a false sole that will fit inside your shoe.

3

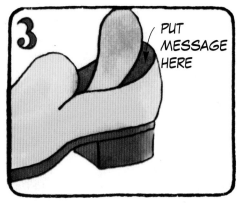

PUT MESSAGE HERE

Slip the message between the real sole and the false sole. Use this method if you think you might be stopped and searched.

1 SECRET POCKET   2

MESSAGE

Cut off the corner of a tea bag and empty out all of the tea. Make two small tabs of sticky tape, like this.

Stick the tea bag in a hidden place, such as the inside of a cap or sleeve. Fold the message very small and tuck it inside.

SPY TRICK

THE SPY IS SEEN STANDING BESIDE THIS WALL. HE SEEMS TO BE INNOCENTLY READING A NEWSPAPER. BUT IS HE?

1 PEN MESSAGE   2

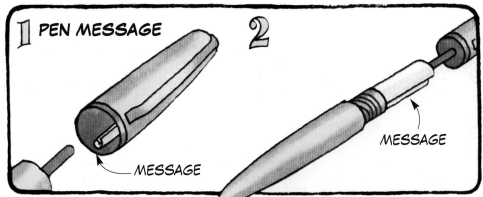

MESSAGE

MESSAGE

Write the message on a small strip of paper. Roll the strip very tightly and keep it hidden in the top of a pen lid.

Alternatively, unscrew a cartridge pen and wind the message strip around the ink cartridge. Then screw the pen together again.

SECRETLY, HE IS HIDING A ROLLED PAPER MESSAGE IN A CRACK IN THE WALL. LATER HIS CONTACT WILL PICK IT UP. TURN THE PAGE TO FIND MORE SPY TRICKS.

Spy post office

A park is a good place to set up a secret post office. Spies often meet or leave messages in parks because you can wander or dawdle in a park without looking too suspicious. Most parks have open places where you can have a good look around to see if you're being followed. And your meetings with other spies can look very innocent and accidental. Follow the spy in the picture here to see some of the ways a spy post office works.

You can hide your messages in all kinds of places if you make sure your contact knows where to look. But if you bury the message, put it in a small plastic container, such as an empty margarine tub or a plastic bottle. This way it won't get rain-soaked or chewed on by a nosy animal.

A good spy tries not to be seen twice in the same spot. Can you work out how a spy could get to all the message spots in the picture without retracing his steps? Clue: the letters on the picture spell the name of a car. Put them in order to find the trail.

Spy language: A place where you leave messages is called a 'drop'.

THE SPY'S CONTACT IS THE MAN SELLING NEWSPAPERS. THE SPY BUYS A PAPER AND FINDS A MESSAGE TUCKED INSIDE.

A

THE SPY STOPS TO PICK A FLOWER NEAR THE RABBIT HOLE. HE SLIPS HIS OTHER HAND INTO THE RABBIT HOLE AND TAKES OUT A TINY BOTTLE WITH A MESSAGE INSIDE.

W

K

THE SPY PICKS UP A NEWSPAPER ON THIS BENCH. THE WORDS UNDERLINED ON THE LEFT-HAND COLUMN ON THE BACK PAGE ARE A SECRET MESSAGE.

S

THE SPY FINDS A MESSAGE PUSHED INTO THE CRACK OF THIS WALL.

WHISPERING WOODS

THE SPY STOPS AND PRETENDS TO SMELL THE FLOWERS. HE FINDS THE MESSAGE IN A SMALL BOTTLE PUSHED INTO THE SOIL.

V

E

G

THE SPY PICKS UP THIS UMBRELLA AND TAKES IT HOME. WHEN HE IS ALONE HE UNSCREWS THE HANDLE AND FINDS A MESSAGE INSIDE.

THE SPY KNEELS BY THIS TREE AND PRETENDS TO TIE HIS SHOELACE. HE FINDS THE MESSAGE UNDERNEATH A TREE ROOT.

N

THE SPY PRETENDS TO STUMBLE AGAINST THIS LOG. HE STOOPS TO RUB HIS SHIN AND PULLS OUT A MESSAGE FROM BENEATH THE LOG.

L

THE SPY SITS DOWN ON THIS BENCH AND FINDS A MESSAGE STUCK UNDER THE BENCH WITH STICKY TAPE.

O

HERE THE SPY MEETS A MAN WALKING A DOG. THE SPY SCRATCHES THE DOG'S HEAD AND FINDS A MESSAGE UNDER THE DOG'S COLLAR.

Quick codes

You can make quick, easy codes by making a few small changes in your messages. The best example is the Word-Split Code. Just split the words in different places to make the message look completely different. For example, 'We trail spies' can be changed to 'Wet rails pies' – all the letters are the same, only the spacing between the letters has changed.

You can make other good codes by changing around the message letters in simple ways or adding dummy letters to the message.

On the right you will find examples of these codes and clues on how to break each kind of code.

FIND THE MASTER SPY

The people you see in the picture below are QZ spies. Each has a message for you in one of the six codes shown on the right. Begin with the message at START – each decoded message will lead you to another contact. Break all the codes to find which of your contacts was actually the Master Spy of the QZ Spy Ring.

BREAKING THE CODES

Try these methods to work out which code was used.

1 Join the first code word to one or two letters of the second word.

2+3 Spell the first few code words, or the whole sentence, backwards.

4 Take away the first letter of each code word and see if the remaining letters make words.

5 Take away the last letter of each code word and see if the remaining letters make words.

6 Exchange the last letter of each word with the first letter of the next.

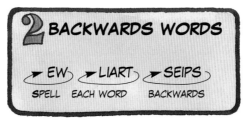

To break the code, join the letters in a different way.

To break the code, spell each code word backwards.

To break the code, spell the sentence backwards.

To break the code, cross out the first letter of each word. Make words from the remaining letters.

To break the code, cross out the last letter of each word. Join up the remaining letters into words.

To break the code, exchange the last letter of each word with the first letter of the next.

Mystery codes

The mysterious papers Black Hat is examining are coded messages. These pages show the key to each of them. Can you decode them?

MUSIC CODE

The key to the music code is at the right. It shows which note stands for each letter of the alphabet and for each of the numbers from one to nine. Use 0 for zero.

Match Black Hat's message notes with those in the key, to find the letter that each note stands for. (The first letter of the message is W.)

A dot marks the end of a word.

1 PIG-PEN CODE

This mysterious-looking code is very easy to use. To make the key, first draw the patterns shown here.

1 RAILFENCE CODE

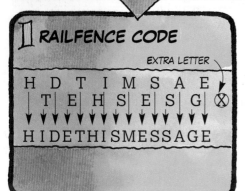

To encode a message, first write the letters in an up-and-down pattern, on two lines. Add a null (extra letter) if needed to make both lines the same length.

2

Now write out the letters of the first line, then the letters of the second line. Put them in groups, to look like words. Make sure your contact knows how to decode this.

3

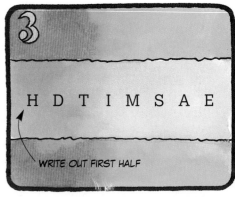

To decode a railfence message, first count out the first half of the message. Write it out with big spaces in between each of the letters.

12

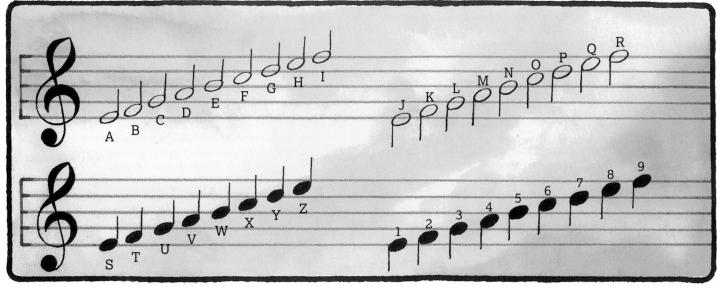

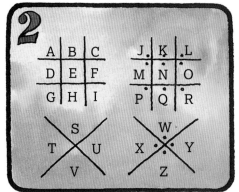

Now write in the letters of the alphabet like this. The pattern of lines or of lines and dots next to each letter is used to stand for that letter.

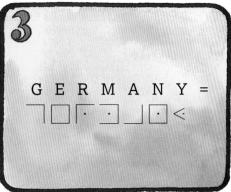

GERMANY =

This example shows how the password 'Germany' looks in Pig-Pen. Now see if you can work out the secret message Black Hat has found.

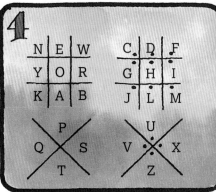

For a more secret Pig-Pen key, write the alphabet in a different order. Start with a keyword (a word with all-different letters), then add the rest of the alphabet.

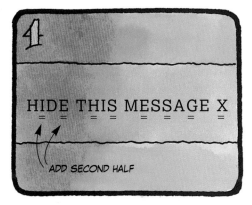

HIDE THIS MESSAGE X

ADD SECOND HALF

Now put the letters of the second half one by one into the spaces, like this. Try this method on the secret message that Black Hat is looking at.

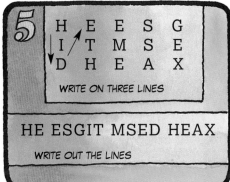

WRITE ON THREE LINES

HE ESGIT MSED HEAX

WRITE OUT THE LINES

To change the code, write the letters in an up-and-down pattern on three lines, like this. Then write out the letters from each line, as before.

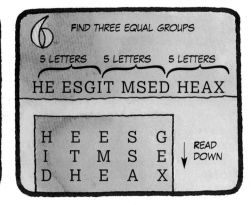

FIND THREE EQUAL GROUPS

5 LETTERS   5 LETTERS   5 LETTERS

HE ESGIT MSED HEAX

READ DOWN

To decode the message your contact must count out three equal groups of letters and write them in three lines again. Then he can read down each group of three.

13

Code machines

With these machines you can encode and decode messages very quickly. The code strip shown below is easy to make. Use it to match the plain alphabet with a code alphabet that starts and finishes at a different letter. For example, start the code alphabet at B. Then change each plain letter for the one that follows it in the alphabet. Change the Zs to As.

To make a code wheel, trace the pattern on page 15. Trace it carefully so that the alphabets line up when you spin the dial.

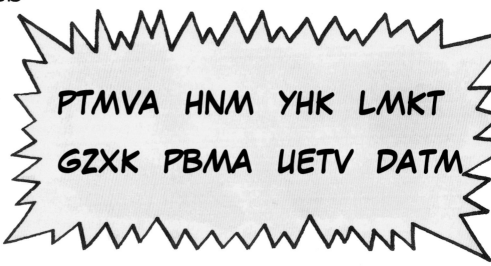

PTMVA HNM YHK LMKT
GZXK PBMA UETV DATM

This message is written in Code T. Match A with T on a code machine to break the code.

When you send messages, be sure your contact knows which code alphabet you have used.

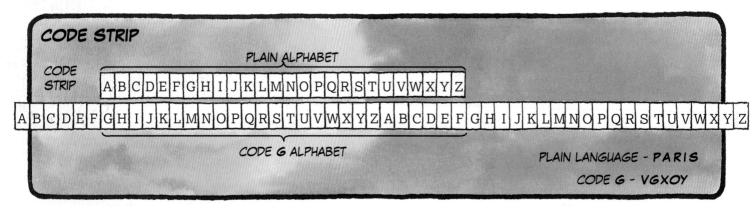

CODE STRIP

CODE STRIP

PLAIN ALPHABET

| A | B | C | D | E | F | G | H | I | J | K | L | M | N | O | P | Q | R | S | T | U | V | W | X | Y | Z |

A B C D E F G H I J K L M N O P Q R S T U V W X Y Z A B C D E F G H I J K L M N O P Q R S T U V W X Y Z

CODE G ALPHABET

PLAIN LANGUAGE - PARIS

CODE G - VGXOY

Mark a strip of paper into 26 spaces, 1cm (½in) wide. Write the alphabet neatly in the spaces. Then mark 52 spaces 1cm/½in wide, on a strip twice as long.

Write the alphabet twice in the long strip, as above. Slide the short strip over the long strip to line up the plain alphabet with a code alphabet.

For example, slide the short strip so that A stands over G to make Code G. Then match each plain letter with the letter beneath it on the code strip.

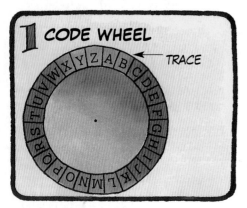

Trace the red wheel from the pattern on page 15. Trace the lines very carefully and mark a dot in the middle of the wheel.

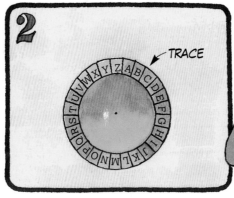

Trace the blue wheel in the same way. Print one letter of the alphabet in each border space, on both wheels. Cut out the wheels.

Draw and cut out some cardboard (such as a cereal box) and glue each paper wheel to a cardboard wheel.

TOP SECRET

This is how to use two code alphabets. First print the message. Then print the names of the alphabets over and over to mark each plain letter. Set the code strip or wheel at P and encode all the letters marked P. Set it at Q to encode the rest. Tell your contact to decode with PQ.

	PQP	QPQPQ	PQP	QPQPQ	PQP
MESSAGE	WHO	WEARS	THE	BLACK	HAT
CODE P	L D	T G	I T	A R	W I
CODE Q	X	M Q I	X	R Q A	Q
CODE PQ	LXD	MTQGI	IXT	RAQRA	WQI

CODE WHEEL PATTERN

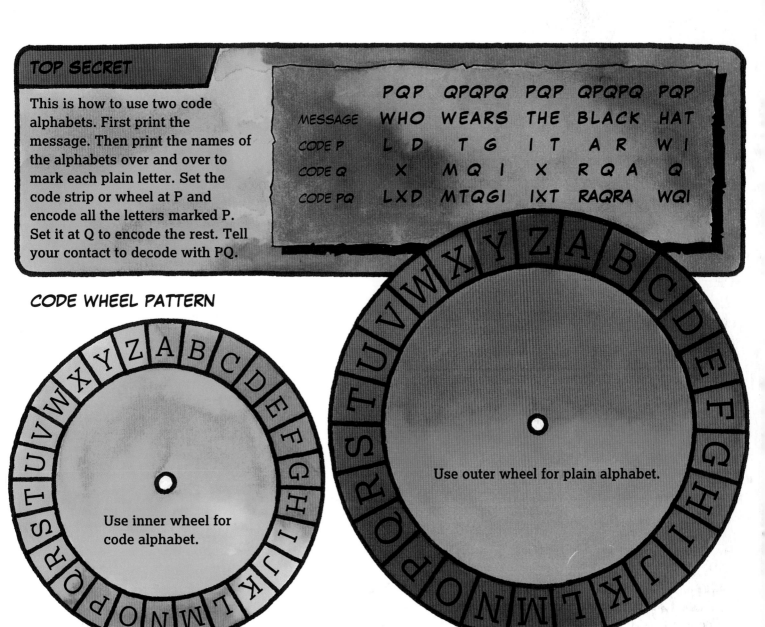

Use inner wheel for code alphabet.

Use outer wheel for plain alphabet.

4 Push a drawing pin or thumbtack through the middle dot of both wheels and into a small hard eraser.

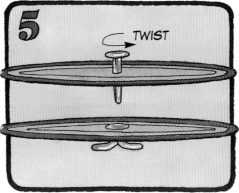

5 TWIST

Alternatively, push a paper fastener through both middle dots. Twist it once to make a hole. Bend out the tabs.

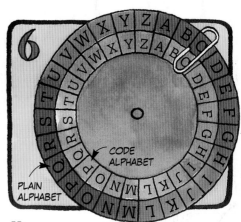

6 CODE ALPHABET

PLAIN ALPHABET

Use a paperclip to hold the wheels in place while you match the plain alphabet with a code alphabet.

15

Black Hat's spy equipment...

Here is Black Hat in his attic den, surrounded by equipment. (You may recognize many of his tools – other pages in the book show you how to make them.) Black Hat has just noticed that someone is climbing towards the attic on a ladder. It may be the window-cleaner – but it may be a spycatcher in disguise.

In the next few minutes Black Hat must find a way to hide all the evidence that he is a spy. How can he do it?

On the next page you can see how the spy den will look in just five minutes. Can you figure out any of the tricks Black Hat uses to hide everything? The answers are on page 17, upside-down.

...and how he hides it away

Where is Black Hat's Spy equipment now? Turn the page upside-down to check your answers.

5 MINUTES LATER

Bottle of invisible ink - inside teapot spout.

Microdot - on the side of the envelope that is turned down. A microdot has a shine that a spycatcher might notice.

Microdot reader in pen barrel - put together as pen.

Code book - hidden in teapot inside small plastic bag with elastic band around it.

Hollow ring - on Black Hat's finger.

Radio – behind sliding panel disguised as bookshelf. The books at the end are real. Those on the right are pieces of book-cover stuck to the panel.

Code Wheel – hidden under lid of sugar bowl.

Binoculars – underneath the teapot cover.

Maps – pushed into sleeves of coat, which are tucked into pockets to keep maps from sliding out.

Invisible writing

A message in secret ink is usually written on the back of an ordinary letter or in the blank spaces between the lines and along the sides.

You will need:

- a piece of white candle
- fine powder for wax writing – you can use powdered instant coffee, chalk scrapings or even fine soil in an emergency.
- ink or paint and a brush or sponge to make the water message appear
- a potato for the potato ink well
- some paper – use thin paper for the water mark
- a toothpick

Always mark the message to show your contact how to develop it (make it appear).

Marks to use are:
wx for a wax message
wm for a water message
h for a message that must be heated
x on the message side of the paper

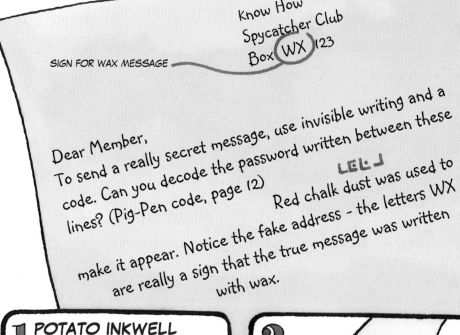

SIGN FOR WAX MESSAGE

Know How
Spycatcher Club
Box WX 123

Dear Member,
To send a really secret message, use invisible writing and a code. Can you decode the password written between these lines? (Pig-Pen code, page 12)
Red chalk dust was used to make it appear. Notice the fake address - the letters WX are really a sign that the true message was written with wax.

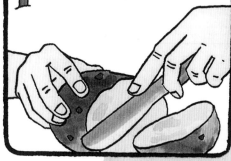

1 POTATO INKWELL

Hold the potato like this and cut off both ends with a table knife, as shown.

Stand the potato on one end. Scoop a hole in the top with a spoon.

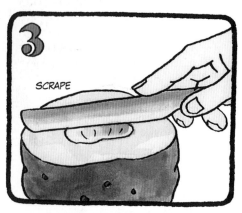

SCRAPE

Now use the blade of the table knife to scrape and squeeze juice from the cut top of the potato into the hole.

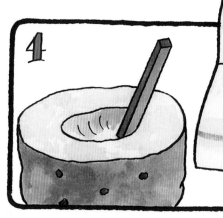

Dip a toothpick into the potato ink to write the message. When the 'ink' dries, the message will be invisible.

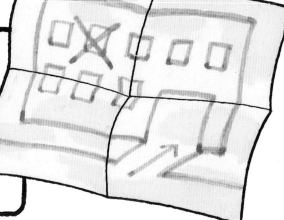

If the message is put in a warm oven (250°F, 120°C, gas mark ½) it will look like this. Make other 'inks' with lemon juice, milk, onion juice or cola.

18

1 WATER WRITING

DRY PAPER
WRITE FIRMLY
WET PAPER

Wet some paper thoroughly. Lay it on a smooth, hard surface. Cover it with dry paper and write firmly. The message will appear on the wet paper when held to the light.

2

The message will vanish when the paper dries and reappear whenever it's wet. Your contact can brush it with watery ink or paint to make it permanent.

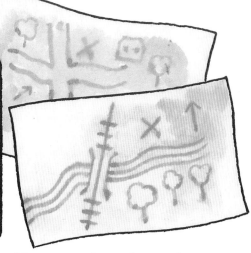

You can make water-mark messages on dry paper with a toothpick dipped in slightly soapy water. The soapy shine will help you see what you're doing.

1 WAX WRITING

PAPER WITH WAXED UNDERSIDE
WRITE FIRMLY
PLAIN PAPER

Wax some paper by rubbing it with a white candle. Lay the waxed side on plain paper. Write firmly to print the message in wax on the paper.

2

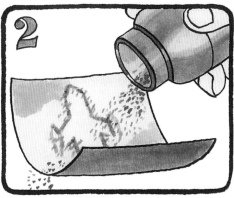

Your contact should sprinkle the message paper with powdered instant coffee or chalk scrapings.

3

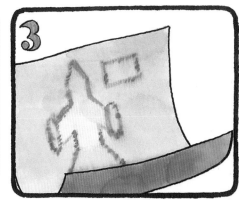

When he gives the paper a gentle shake the powder will stick to the message and slide off the rest of the paper.

SPY TRICK

BLACK HAT HAD JUST ARRIVED AT THE AIRPORT. HE WAS STOPPED AND SEARCHED, BUT WAS FOUND TO BE CARRYING ONLY... A SEWING KIT...

THE SPY WAS ALLOWED TO GO. AFTER ALL, A FEW NEEDLES AND THREADS CAN'T BE MUCH HELP TO THE ENEMY... OR CAN THEY?

ALONE IN HIS ROOM, THE SPY DREW THE THREAD OVER A HOT LIGHT BULB, AND TINY DOTS OF INVISIBLE INK APPEARED ALONG IT. IT WAS ANOTHER CODE

Spotting clues

A spy must be very good at spotting clues. He has to get information from little signs and marks that other people would not notice. This page shows how to get information from footprints and from car and cycle tracks. This can be very useful if you lose sight of someone you are following. Sometimes the person you are following may disguise herself. Watch out for clues that can help you see through the disguise. Try the Spy Test below to see how good you are at spotting this kind of clue.

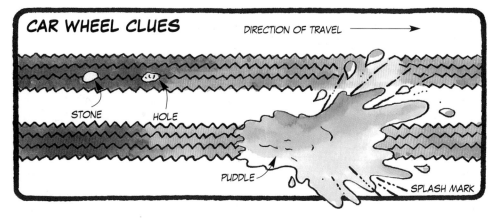

CAR WHEEL CLUES

DIRECTION OF TRAVEL →

STONE
HOLE
PUDDLE
SPLASH MARK

A stone hit by a car wheel is pressed down to make a hole and then kicked back. The marks left in the road show the direction in which the car was going.

When a wheel hits a puddle it splashes the oil or water forwards. Look for the splash-mark to work out which way the wheel was going.

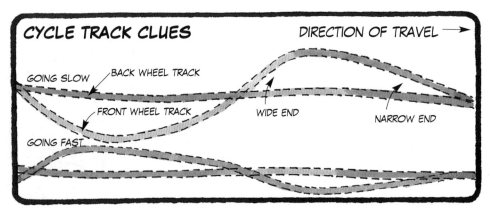

CYCLE TRACK CLUES

DIRECTION OF TRAVEL →

GOING SLOW
BACK WHEEL TRACK
FRONT WHEEL TRACK
WIDE END
NARROW END
GOING FAST

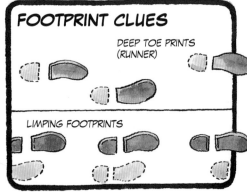

FOOTPRINT CLUES

DEEP TOE PRINTS (RUNNER)

LIMPING FOOTPRINTS

The front wheel of a cycle makes a loopy track, because the cyclist has to keep his or her balance. They turn less when going fast and make smaller loops.

After turning the wheel, the cyclist straightens it, so the loops are always wider at one end than the other. The narrow end points out where he or she is heading.

If the person you are trailing is running, look for a deep toe print and light heel print. If they are limping, look for a deep footprint and then a light footprint.

SPY TEST

SPY Z KNOWS MANY DISGUISE TRICKS. BUT HE FORGETS TO HIDE ONE CLUE. READ ON AND SEE IF YOU CAN SPOT IT.

BLACK HAT HAS JUST SPOTTED SPY Z NEAR THE PALM HOTEL.

AS SPY Z ENTERS THE HOTEL AND CALLS THE ELEVATOR, BLACK HAT IS WATCHING. NOW IS HIS CHANCE TO SEE WHERE Z HIDES OUT.

WHEN SPY Z ENTERS THE ELEVATOR BLACK HAT RUNS UPSTAIRS...

SLAM!

Trapping spies

Suppose you think that your enemy is getting into your secret hiding places. Set up one of the spy traps on this page and the intruder will be tricked into making noise or leaving a clue that shows someone has been there. Door Trap No. 2 is particularly useful. Made with flour, it leaves a mark on anyone who goes through the door.

You can make another good noise trap by sprinkling sugar on the floor. But people in socks or soft soles can avoid this trap.

HALLWAY TRAP

Tape a thin black thread from wall to wall, like this. Anyone who walks past this spot will make the thread fall down.

DESK TRAP

CLUE MARK

Spread some papers in a careless-looking way. Draw a tiny line that runs across two of them, like this. The smallest movement of the papers will break the line.

DOOR TRAP NO.1

GLUED HAIR (GLUE IT LOW DOWN OR HIGH UP)

Glue a hair across the opening crack, like this. Check later – if someone has gone through the door, the hair will come unglued. Use the same trap on a drawer.

DOOR TRAP NO. 2

FILL

TAPE

THREAD

Find a very small cardboard box. Fill it with beans (for a noise trap) or with flour (for a marking trap).

Tape one end of a thread to the box and prop it on a door frame. Tape the thread to the door, like this, and close the door. When someone opens it, the box will fall.

...AND REACHES THE FIRST FLOOR LANDING JUST IN TIME TO SEE A SECOND PERSON ENTER THE ELEVATOR.

ON THE NEXT FLOOR, TWO MEN GET OUT. THIS IS THE TOP FLOOR - ONE OF THEM MUST BE SPY 2 IN DISGUISE.

BLACK HAT FOLLOWS THE TWO MEN DOWN THE HALL. AS THEY TAKE OUT THEIR KEYS HE SEES THE CLUE THAT HE'S BEEN WAITING FOR. DO YOU? (SEE PAGE 25 TO FIND THE ANSWER)

Silent signals

If you and your contact can see each other but cannot speak or get close enough to pass a message, signal with the silent alphabet shown on the page on the right. Or blink the Morse code as shown below and on page 24. In a crowded room or busy street you and your contact can send quick messages or warnings with silent hand and leg signals.

SILENT HAND AND LEG SIGNALS

1 Hand in pocket – yes.

2 Hands in pockets – no.

3 Scratching head – can you meet me at the hiding place?

4 Scratching back of neck – be careful. You're being watched.

5 Crossing legs – leave your message at the 'drop'.

6 Both hands behind back – I can't pass the message now.

7 Scratching ear – I will telephone you later.

8 On one leg with hand in pocket – I'm going home.

MORSE BLINK SIGNALS   MORSE WINK SIGNALS

Blink for a count of one to make a dot and blink for a count of three to make a dash. A stare means the end of a word or message.

Wink to make a dot and blink to make a dash. A stare means the end of a word or message.

Silent alphabet

On this page you can see how to make the letters of the alphabet with your hands. The pictures show how the hand signals should look to your contact. Don't try this in front of a mirror – the reflected signals will be the wrong way around. You and your contact could try doing the signals together to get them right.

At the bottom of the page you'll find quick signs to answer questions or to show whether or not you understand.

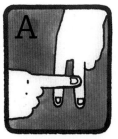 A
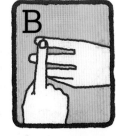 B
 C
 D

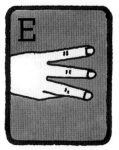 E
 F
 G
 H

 I
 J
 K
 L
 M
 N

 O
 P
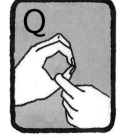 Q
 R
 S
 T

 U
 V
 W
 X
 Y
 Z

QUICK SIGNS

 YES
 NO
 UNDERSTOOD
 NOT UNDERSTOOD
 REPEAT

Morse code

Morse is a particularly useful code because it can be sent in so many different ways. You can signal it with a buzzer or a whistle or by flashing a light on a dark night. Morse can also be tapped out or blinked with your eyes. This page shows the Morse code alphabet.

In this code (●) stands for a short signal and a dash (–) stands for a long signal. To time the signals correctly, remember that a dash is always three times as long as a dot. For example, you should flash your light for a count of one to make a dot and for a count of three to make a dash.

Don't run the letters or words together. Between two letters, wait for a count of three. Between two words, wait for a count of five. Use the extra signals shown below to make sure that your contact is ready to receive your message and that he understands it.

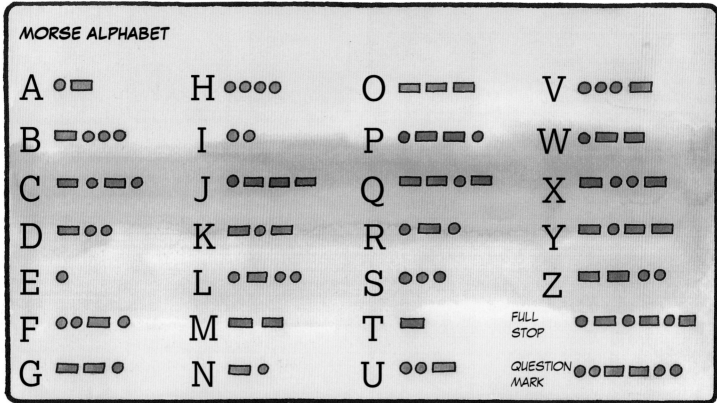

MORSE ALPHABET

A ● ▬
B ▬ ● ● ●
C ▬ ● ▬ ●
D ▬ ● ●
E ●
F ● ● ▬ ●
G ▬ ▬ ●

H ● ● ● ●
I ● ●
J ● ▬ ▬ ▬
K ▬ ● ▬
L ● ▬ ● ●
M ▬ ▬
N ▬ ●

O ▬ ▬ ▬
P ● ▬ ▬ ●
Q ▬ ▬ ● ▬
R ● ▬ ●
S ● ● ●
T ▬
U ● ● ▬

V ● ● ● ▬
W ● ▬ ▬
X ▬ ● ● ▬
Y ▬ ● ▬ ▬
Z ▬ ▬ ● ●

FULL STOP ● ▬ ● ▬ ● ▬
QUESTION MARK ● ● ▬ ▬ ● ●

SENDER'S SIGNALS

● ▬ ▬ ● ▬

This means 'I'm about to send a message'. Wait for the receiver to signal 'ready' before you start.

● ● ▬

This means 'end of message'. If the receiver answers 'not understood', repeat the message.

● ● ● ● ● ● ●

This means 'mistake'. When you have misspelled a word, repeat the word.

RECEIVER'S SIGNALS

● ▬

This means 'ready to receive'. At the end of a message it means 'message understood'.

● ● ● ● ● ● ●

This means 'not ready to receive'. At the end of a message it means 'message not understood'.

Quick signal code

This is a special code to use for signalling if you don't have time to learn the whole Morse alphabet. With this code you can send any message with just six signals.

The code is made with an alphabet box. Each plain letter is replaced by the two code letters that line up with it in the frame of the box. There are six different code letters in the frame. They are written in capitals at the side and in small letters at the top of the box. The code pair should start with a capital. For example, the code pair used for R is Oi.

Learn the Morse or semaphore signals for the six letters used. Encode the message before you start signalling. Your contact should write down the code message as he receives it and decode it later.

To make the code more secret, start the plain alphabet with a keyword, like 'crazy'. Then add the other letters of the alphabet.

TELEPHONE MESSAGES

You can read off the code pairs like this. Say 'adle' for A, 'eedle' for E, 'idle' for I, 'odle' for O, 'yewdle' for U, and 'wydle' for Y.

If you turn the coded message into Morse you can read it out by saying 'iddy' for a dot and 'umpty' for a dash. Remember to wait for a count of three between two letters. Between two words, wait for a count of five.

ALPHABET BOX

CODE LETTERS	e	a	i	o	u
E	A	B	C	D	E
A	F	G	H	I	J
I	K	L	M	N	O
O	P	Q	R	S	T
U	U	V	W	X	Y
Y	Z				

Replace each plain letter with the capital letter on its row and the small letter on its column.

Always start with a capital. For example, the code pair for R is Oi.

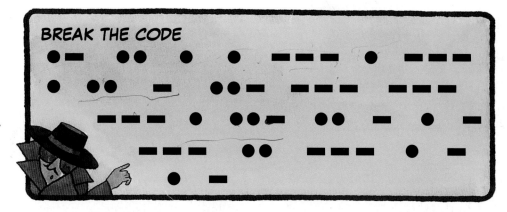

BREAK THE CODE

HERE IS A MESSAGE BLACK HAT HAS JUST ENCODED, READY FOR SIGNALLING. CAN YOU BREAK THE CODE?

REMEMBER – THE FIRST LETTER OF EACH CODE PAIR COMES FROM THE SIDE OF THE BOX.

Quick disguises

These quick disguises can help you fool your enemy. If your enemy is following at a distance he will keep track of you by watching for something special about the way that you look. Start out with a disguise that will catch his eye. Wear a bright scarf or a sling or use a special walk (see below). Then go into a building or duck into a doorway and come out without it. Your enemy will be left wondering where you've gone.

Spy language:
Following is known as 'shadowing' or 'trailing'. The person who does it is a 'tail' or a 'shadow'.

CHANGE YOUR WALK

A good spy trick is to pretend you have a stiff leg or a limp. But you might forget your stiff leg, or start limping on the wrong foot. Here are some ways to make sure that you remember.

1   To make yourself limp, put a small stone in one shoe.
2   For a stiff leg, put a ruler at the back of one knee and tie it on with a scarf. Then you won't be able to bend it. Wear something long to hide the ruler.

ARM IN SLING

You will need a helper to put your arm in a sling. Use a big scarf or a piece of cloth folded like this. Hold your arm across it and put a corner around your neck. Lift the bottom corner and knot it to the piece around your neck. Then pin the side cover over your elbow, as shown.

ONE-ARMED SPY

ARM INSIDE COAT

SLEEVE IN POCKET

Wear your coat like this to look as though you only have one arm. Put one arm into a sleeve. Tuck the other sleeve into a pocket. Button the coat with one arm inside.

TWO-WAY SCARF

KNOT THREAD

TAKE OUT PINS AFTER STITCHING

To make a quick-change scarf you will need two scarves the same size and shape but different shades or patterns. Pin them together like this and stitch around all four sides.

CHANGE YOUR SHAPE

1

PUT ON TOWEL

WITH DISGUISE

WITHOUT DISGUISE

HAT AND TOWEL IN BAG

To raise your shoulders, lay a small towel behind your neck, like this. Then put a coat on over it. This will help you look like an older person with muscular shoulders. To change your back view even more, wear a hat or scarf as well. Take a folded plastic bag in your pocket. Later you can carry the hat and towel in the bag.

2

To make yourself look fatter, tie a small cushion around your middle. Button a coat on over it, or wear a very big sweater.

Jokes & Tricks

Making a magic wand

A wand is a useful thing to have when you do magic tricks. You can wave it when you say the magic words or push it through things to show they are empty.

If you point your wand at something, the people watching will look at it. Then you can do a trick without them noticing the secret part.

You can buy a wand from a magic shop or make one of your own. Here is an easy way to make a magic wand.

PAPER WAND

Cut out a piece of thick black paper, about 30 x 10cm (12 x 4in). Roll it around two pencils (a) and glue the edge to make a tube.

When the glue is dry, shake out the pencils. Cut two strips of white paper, each about 2 x 8cm (1 x 3in). Glue one around each end (b).

STICKY WAND

MY MAGIC WAND STICKS TO MY HAND!

THE SECRET

PIN BETWEEN FINGERS

Push a pin into the wand (a). Hold the pin between your fingers (b) so no one can see it. Pull out the pin secretly so no one else can do the trick.

BALANCING WAND

1

CUT A SLIT

BENT KNITTING NEEDLE

You need a long, thin knitting needle and a paper wand. Cut a slit near one end. Bend over one end of the knitting needle.

2

APPLE

SLIT

NEEDLE

Push the needle into the slit in the wand. For the trick, hide the slit in one hand. Try to balance an apple on top of the wand.

3

PUSH UP NEEDLE

Now push up the bent end of the needle so the point sticks into the apple. Wave the wand and the apple will stick to it.

4

WHEN I SAY THE MAGIC WORDS I CAN BALANCE THE APPLE!

Pull the end of the needle down again so the point disappears. Take the apple off and show everyone the tip of the wand.

When does an astronaut have his midday meal?   At launch time!

Table tricks

READY-SLICED BANANA

1 HERE IS AN ORDINARY BANANA.

2 WITH MY MAGIC WAND I SLICE IT IN BITS WITHOUT CUTTING THE SKIN.

3 WHEN I PEEL THE BANANA IT IS SLICED INTO BITS!

THE SECRET

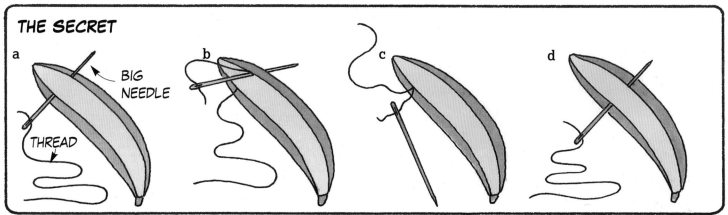

a BIG NEEDLE
THREAD

b

c

d

Push a piece of strong thread, about 20cm (8in) long, through the eye of a big needle. Push the needle through one flat side of a big banana (a).

Pull the needle out, leaving the thread under the skin. Now push the needle back through the same hole and under the next flat side (b). Keep going all the way around.(c).

When you reach the first hole, pull the two ends of the thread. This will cut the banana inside the skin. Make more cuts in the same way down the whole banana (d).

MAGIC STRAW

PIN

TAKE THE PIN OUT WHEN YOU'VE MADE THE HOLE.

FINGER AND THUMB OVER HOLE

SINGING GLASSES

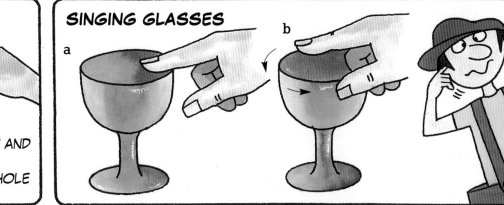

a

b

Make a hole in a drinking straw with a pin. When someone tries to drink with it, they will just suck up air. When you drink with it, put your fingers over the holes.

You can make a glass sing a long whining tune. Put a little water in the glass. Dip one finger in the water and rub it gently around the top edge of the glass (a).

If it does not work at once, try rubbing harder or more gently. Keep your finger just on the rim (b). Thin glasses work better than thick ones. Try lots of different ones.

Why do witches fly about on broomsticks?   ¡Ʌʌɐǝɥ oo⊥ ǝɹɐ sɹǝuɐǝ|ɔ ɯnnɔɐʌ ǝsnɐɔǝꓭ

Finger tricks

These Finger tricks are great fun to do. When you play them, you can pretend you are hurt. With the Wounded Finger, just wear the bandage until someone notices. Then pretend you are very brave.

The Wand Through Head Trick takes a few tries to get right. Try it secretly in front of a mirror until it looks right. You can pull the wand out of your head again. Just hold the wand in place with your other hand. Then slide the paper back along the wand.

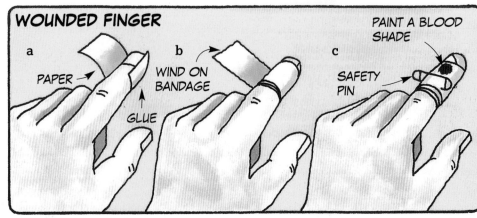

WOUNDED FINGER

a — PAPER — GLUE

b — WIND ON BANDAGE

c — PAINT A BLOOD SHADE — SAFETY PIN

Wrap a piece of white paper around one finger (a). Stick it with glue. Wind on a short piece of bandage, going over the top of the finger as well (b).

Paint a part of the bandage red with a little brown to look like dried blood (c). Slide off the bandage. Put it on secretly when you want to fool someone.

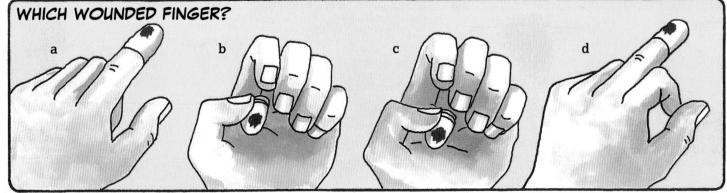

WHICH WOUNDED FINGER?

a   b   c   d

Make a Wounded Finger bandage just big enough to go on the top of one finger (a). To change it to another finger, bend the finger over into your palm (b).

Hold the bandage with your thumb and slide it off (c). Slide the bandage onto the next finger. Open your hand to show that a different finger is hurt (d).

Try sliding the bandage off and on quickly. You can move it to all your fingers, one at a time. Pretend you can't remember which finger has the wound.

SHAKY HAND

Hold out your hand to shake hands with someone. When they take it, off it comes.

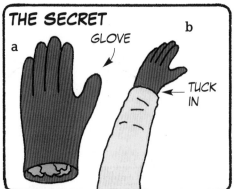

THE SECRET

a — GLOVE — b — TUCK IN

Stuff the fingers and palm of a glove with paper towels or bits of material. Make sure the fingers look full and fat (a). Hold the glove by the open end. Pull down your sleeve to hide your hand (b).

MISSING FINGER

Pull on a glove, putting two fingers into one space. This leaves an empty glove finger which you can wiggle around in a horrible floppy way.

Which trees do fingers and thumbs grow on?   Palm trees!

1 LIVING FINGER

CUT OUT

Find a small cardboard box with a hinged lid. Cut a hole, big enough for your finger to go through, in the bottom of the box.

2

HOLE   COTTON WOOL BALLS

Glue cotton wool balls to the bottom of the box. Put it around the hole but not over it. Close the box before you show anyone the finger.

3

Hold the box in one hand, like this. Then, as you open the box, quickly push one finger through the hole and bend it over. Keep it still and then wiggle it.

STRING THROUGH FINGER TRICK

IT DOESN'T HURT MUCH IF I DO IT SLOWLY!

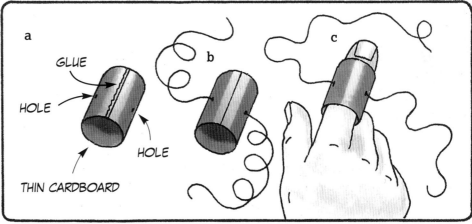

a   GLUE
HOLE
HOLE
THIN CARDBOARD
b
c

Cut out a piece of thin cardboard about 7 x 4cm (3 x 1 ½in) wide. Roll it into a tube and glue the edges together (a). Make a hole in each side of the tube.

Push a piece of string, about 50cm (20in) long, through the holes (b). Slide the tube on to one finger (c). Slowly pull one end of the string. Then pull the other end.

WAND THROUGH HEAD TRICK

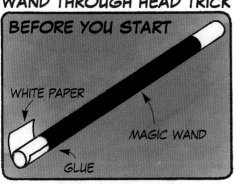

BEFORE YOU START

WHITE PAPER

MAGIC WAND

GLUE

Wrap a small piece of white paper around one end of a wand with two white ends. Glue it together but make sure that you can still slide it up and down the wand.

1

Hold the end of the wand that has the paper on it. Put the other end to your head, behind one ear. Make sure the back of your hand is towards the people watching you.

2

Now push the piece of paper very slowly along the wand so that the wand looks as if it is going into your head. The real end of the wand is hidden behind your hand.

What's worse than a giraffe with a sore throat?   A centipede with sore feet!

31

Disappearing and appearing

VANISHING WATER

Make this magazine a magic one and use it to make water vanish. When you have done the trick, put the magazine down so it is upright and pour out the water when no one is looking. You can use the magazine lots of times for making other things appear or disappear.

The magazine should be thick but floppy and make sure there are no holes in the plastic bag.

BEFORE YOU START

Spread glue on the top edges of a small plastic bag. Press the bag to an inside page of a magazine. Close the magazine and press the pages together. Leave to dry.

HOW IT LOOKS

HERE IS AN ORDINARY MAGAZINE. YOU CAN SEE THE INSIDE AND THE OUTSIDE.

I ROLL IT INTO A CONE AND STIR IT WITH MY MAGIC WAND.

I POUR IN SOME WATER AND SAY THE MAGIC WORDS.

I UNROLL THE MAGAZINE AND THE WATER HA[S] DISAPPEARED!

1 THE SECRET

OPEN THE BAG WITH THE WAND

Roll the magazine into a cone. Push one end of a magic wand into the pages where the plastic bag is. Waggle the wand around to open the top of the bag, like this.

2

POUR WATER INTO THE BAG

Pour about half a cup of water into the bag. If you pour in just a little and then a little more and then a little more, it will look like quite a lot of water.

3

HOLD UP MAGAZINE

Unroll the magazine and hold it up by the top corners. Show the inside and outside. Close it and put it down so it stands upright or the water will run out.

1 VANISHING COIN

CURL OF STICKY TAPE

Make a small curl of sticky tape, like this, so the sticky side is on the outside. Press it down in the corner of a small scarf or bright handkerchief.

2

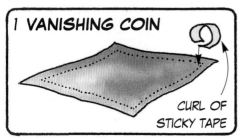

COIN *TAPE HIDDEN IN HAND* *FOLD OVER CORNERS*

a   b   c   d

Cover the sticky tape with one hand and ask someone to put a small coin on the scarf (a). Fold over the corner and press the tape down onto the coin (b).

Fold over the other three corners, like this (c). Pick up the first corner, covering the coin with your hand (d). Show that the coin has disappeared from the scarf.

What sort of lighting did Noah put in the Ark?   ¡ƃuᴉʇɥƃᴉl poolℲ

EMPTY TUBE

Use a big empty tube to make things appear out of the air. This trick cannot be done too close to other people or they will see how it works. When you have finished the trick, stand the tube up on end so no one can see where things come from.

YOU WILL NEED

- 2 pieces of thick black paper, about 25 x 25cm (10 x 10in)
- glue
- bright tissues or thin paper

1 HOW IT LOOKS

HERE IS AN ABSOLUTELY EMPTY TUBE. YOU CAN SEE THERE IS NOTHING IN IT.

2

I SAY THE MAGIC WORDS AND SUDDENLY, LOTS OF THINGS APPEAR!

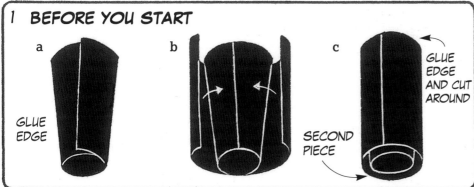

1 BEFORE YOU START

a

GLUE EDGE

b

c

GLUE EDGE AND CUT AROUND

SECOND PIECE

Roll one piece of black paper into a tube. Make it slightly wider at one end (a). Stick the edge with glue. Spread glue around the top of the wider end.

Wrap the second piece of paper around the first tube (b). Glue the edges exactly together to make the second tube straight. Cut off the parts at the top (c).

2

TUCK IN THIN PIECES OF PAPER

To get the trick ready, push small pieces of bright or thin paper down between the two tubes. Hold this end towards you so no one can see the secret space.

1 MAKING COOKIES

a GLUE b COOKIES

Open a thick, floppy magazine in the middle. Glue the pages together around the edges and bottom (a). When the glue is dry, put some cookies in one side (b).

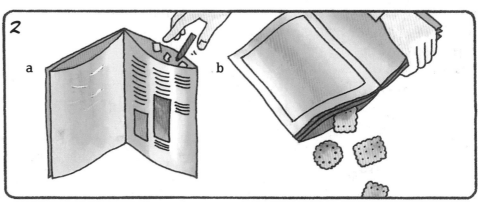

2

a

b

To do the trick, let everyone see you put some things, such as pieces of paper and pencils, into the magazine. Close the magazine.

Now say the magic words or wave your wand. Open the magazine again and tip out the cookies. Be careful to hold the other side so the things don't drop out.

What's green, hairy and goes up and down?   A gooseberry in a lift!

Cutting and mending magic

Here are two easy ways to cut string in half and then make it into one piece again. All you need are pieces of string and a pair of scissors.

For the Tearing Trick, you will need two small paper napkins, which look exactly alike, and some glue.

When you do the tricks, look at your hands as if you really expect some magic to happen. And remember to say the magic words each time.

1 HOW IT LOOKS

HERE IS A PERFECTLY ORDINARY PIECE OF STRING. I CUT IT IN HALF.

2

I SAY THE MAGIC WORD AND IT IS IN ONE PIECE AGAIN!

1 THE SECRET

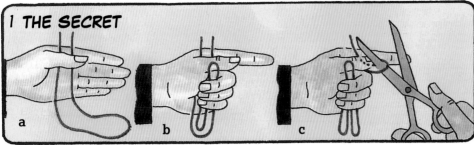

a b c

Hold the ends of the string in one hand (a). Bring up the loop and hold it with your fingers (b).

Hook one blade of the scissors under one string near the end (c). Pretend you are hooking the loop.

2

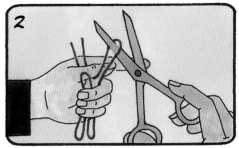

Pull the string up above your hand so it can be seen. Cut the string very slowly and obviously.

3

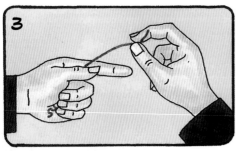

Hold one bit of the string you have cut. Push all the rest of the string into your hand and hold it.

4

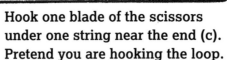

Say the magic words. Pull the string very slowly out of your hand to show it is in one piece.

5

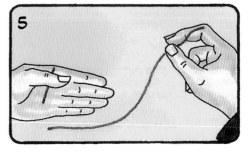

Keep the short cut-off string in your hand. Hide it in your pocket when no one is looking.

1 STRING ALONG

a — SMALL LOOP b

Hide a short loop of string in your hand (a). Let everyone see you hold a long piece (b).

2

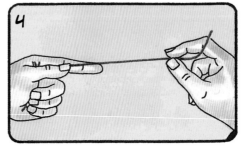

Hook one blade of the scissors under the short loop and pull it up a bit. Cut it in half.

3

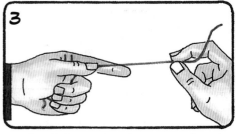

Push all the string into your hand. Hold one end of the long piece and pull it out. Hide the short bits.

What is an astronaut's watch called?

A lunartick!

34

TEARING TRICK

BEFORE YOU START

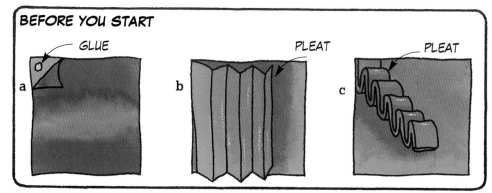

GLUE

a

PLEAT

b

PLEAT

c

Put two paper napkins, which look exactly the same, on top of each other. Dab a bit of glue on to one corner (a) and stick them together.

Fold the top napkin to make pleats (b). Then pleat that strip up (c) to make a neat square in one corner. The trick is ready!

VANISHING KNOT

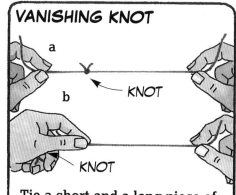

a

KNOT

b

KNOT

Tie a short and a long piece of string together (a). Put all the string in one hand. Pull out one end, sliding the knot along and hiding it in your hand (b).

HOW IT LOOKS

1

HERE IS A PAPER NAPKIN I TEAR IT INTO VERY SMALL PIECES.

2

I PUT THE PIECES INTO MY HAND. NOW I WHISPER THE MAGIC WORDS.

3

SLOWLY, VERY SLOWLY, I PULL THE NAPKIN OUT OF MY HAND!

THE SECRET

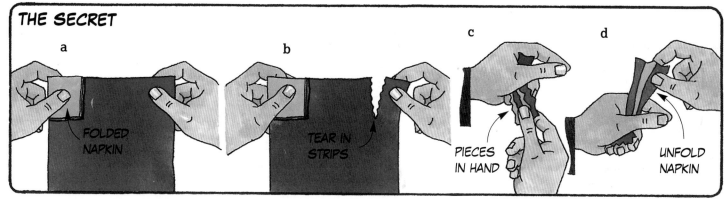

a

FOLDED NAPKIN

b

TEAR IN STRIPS

c

PIECES IN HAND

d

UNFOLD NAPKIN

Hold up the napkins with one thumb over the folded-up square napkin (a). Use your hand to tear the unfolded napkin into strips (b).

Tear the strips into even smaller pieces. Put all the pieces into one hand (c). Put your hand to your mouth and say the magic words.

Holding the top corner of the folded-up napkin, pull it slowly out of your hand (d). Hide the torn-up pieces in your other hand.

What has a bottom at its top?

¡A leg!

Clever card tricks

There are hundreds of card tricks. Some are very difficult and need lots of practice. Here are some easy ones that are fun to do. All you need is a pack of ordinary playing cards.

Try to talk while you're doing card tricks. It stops people from thinking about what you're doing and puzzling out your secrets. With the Pick a Card tricks, ask the person to look hard at the chosen card. While they're staring, they won't notice what you're doing.

CRAZY CARD

When you do this trick make the card follow the wand. Move the wand up and down slowly, then quickly, then in little jerks.

THE SECRET

Hold some cards facing you, like this. Wave your wand over the cards. Then move your thumb up and down to make one card move.

READING FINGER TRICK

Hold out some cards and ask a friend to pick one (a) without you seeing it. Take it, like this (b) and rub it with one finger. Say you are reading it.

Put the card back in the pack and hold it together neatly (a). Now lift off some cards. The one that comes face up is the card you rubbed with your finger (b).

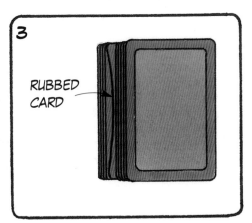

The secret is that when you rub the card, you bend it a little. When it's in the pack, it holds the cards apart and you can lift them off at the right place every time.

MAGIC SEVENS

This really is a magic card trick. It comes right every time you do it. You need 21 cards. Any 21 will do but make sure they are all from the same pack.

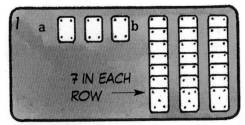

Put down three cards face-up in a line (a). Add a second card to each row in the line, then a third, until you have used them all (b). Ask someone to look at the rows, choose a card, but not say it out loud.

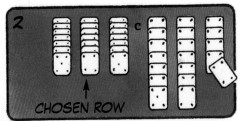

Ask them which row their card is in. Gather the cards into stacks and put them all together with the stack with the chosen card in it in between the other two. Then, lay out the cards, face-up in three rows, as before (c).

Why did the chicken cross the road?

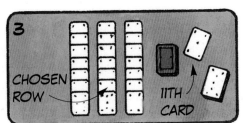

Ask which row the chosen card is now in. Gather the cards again as you did in step 2. Keeping the cards in the same order, turn them over. From the top, count out ten cards. The eleventh is the chosen one.

For fowl reasons!

PICK A CARD

LOOK AT THIS ONE

PICKED CARD

Fan out some cards (a). Ask a friend to pick one and look at it, without you seeing it.

Take half the pack in your right hand and look, secretly, at the bottom card (b).

Ask a friend to put back the picked card, face-down, on the cards in your left hand (c). Put the right-hand stack on top.

Turn them over, from the top, one at a time. The card after the one you looked at will be the picked card (d).

PICK ANOTHER CARD

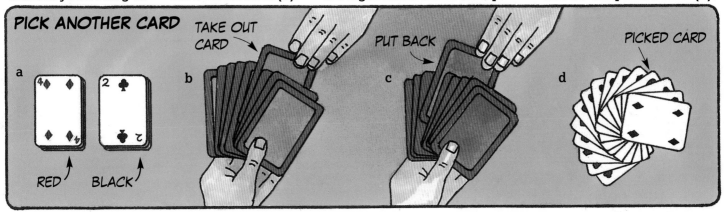

TAKE OUT CARD

PUT BACK

PICKED CARD

RED   BLACK

Before you do this trick, divide a pack of cards into red and black ones (a). Put the two halves together again. Fan them out, face down. Ask someone to pick one.

Hold one edge of the fan towards the person so they take a card from one end (b). Ask them to put it back. Move the fan around so it goes in at the other end (c).

Turn the cards over and hold them up so no one else can see them. If the picked card is red, it will be among the black cards (d). If it is black, it will be with the reds.

1 CARD THROUGH CARDS

Hold a pack of cards in one hand. Pick off the top two cards, holding the edges exactly together so they look like one card. Let everyone see which card it is.

2

Put the two cards down on top of the pack. Slide off the top one (a) and put it at the bottom of the pack (b). Let everyone see very clearly what you are doing.

3

Give the pack a good bang with one hand (a). Say that this is to bang the bottom card up to the top again. Pick off the top card and show it is the same one again (b).

What do you get if you cross a kangaroo with an elephant?   Huge holes all over Australia!

Crafty coin tricks

VANISHING COIN

1

"WATCH THIS CAREFULLY. I'M GOING TO PRESS THIS COIN INTO YOUR HAND THREE TIMES."

Ask a friend to sit down facing you and hold out one hand. Hold a coin between your fingers and thumb. Press it into the friend's hand but keep hold of it.

2

"THE THIRD TIME I WANT YOU TO GRAB IT FROM ME."

Lift your hand above your head. Then press the coin into the hand again. The third time ask the friend to grab it. But the coin has vanished. Show your empty hand.

3 THE SECRET

When you raise your hand the third time, drop the coin on to the top of your head. Pretend you are still holding it and press the friend's hand hard with one finger.

---

1 MAGIC SPINNER

Hold a big coin upright on a table with one finger, like this. Now rub that finger with a finger of the other hand and explain you are working up the magic.

2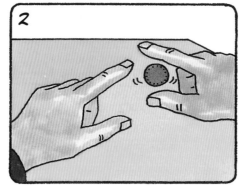

Now quickly run your finger along towards the nail. Lift up both hands and the coin spins away from you.

THE SECRET

When you do the last rub of your finger, whizz your hand away and just catch the edge of the coin with your thumb. This is to make it spin. Try it in secret.

---

1 DETECTIVE WORK

TOPS
SMALL COIN

Put three small bottle tops, all exactly the same, down on a table. Give someone a small coin and ask him to hide it under one top while you look the other way.

2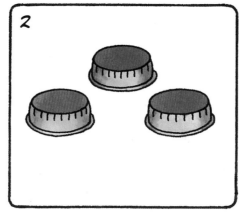

When the coin has been hidden, stare very hard at each top. Then pick up the one hiding the coin. You will be right every time.

THE SECRET

GLUE
HAIR

Before you do this trick, pull out a hair from your head. Glue about 3cm (1in) of it to a coin, like this. When the coin is under a top, look for the hair sticking out under it.

What cake tried to take over the world? Attila the Bun!

38

DISSOLVING COIN

1 HERE IS A COIN AND MY MAGIC SCARF.

2 I HIDE THE COIN IN THE SCARF.

3 NOW I PICK UP A GLASS OF WATER.

4 I PUT THE SCARF OVER THE GLASS AND DROP THE COIN IN.

5 I TAKE AWAY THE SCARF AND YOU CAN SEE THE PENNY.

6 I COVER THE GLASS AGAIN WITH THE SCARF AND SAY THE MAGIC WORDS...

7 WHEN I TAKE AWAY THE SCARF THE COIN HAS DISAPPEARED!

1 THE SECRET
TILT GLASS
DROP COIN

2
COIN UNDER THE GLASS

3
COIN HIDDEN IN HAND

When you cover the glass with the scarf, tilt the glass a little. Drop the coin so it hits the outside of the glass and falls into your hand.

Before you take the scarf away, make sure the coin is under the glass. It will then look as if it is in the glass.

When you take away the scarf, hide the coin in your hand. Hold up the glass with your fingers and thumb. You can hide the coin later.

What's worse than finding a maggot in an apple?   Finding half a maggot!

39

Putting on a show

When you're good at doing magic, try putting on a show for your friends. Before a show, try out all the tricks a few times in front of a mirror. Then you can see exactly how they look.

Write out a list of your tricks and put it on the table. It will remind you of the order you've decided to do them. Put all the things you need on the table. Have a box beside it so you can drop things into it when you have done the tricks. Start and end the show with two of your very best tricks. Arrange the others so each one looks very different from the last. Do not do two that look a bit alike.

If you find it easy, talk to the audience while you're doing the tricks. If this is hard for you, put on some music, just loud enough for people to hear.

It's a good idea to have an assistant to help you and hand you the things you need. Choose a friend who will keep your magic tricks secret.

MAKING MISTAKES

When you're putting on a show, don't worry if a trick goes wrong. Just pretend it's part of the show and no one will notice. It is a good idea to have a whistle or something which makes a noise. This startles the audience and you can go on to the next trick. Or you can do a quick trick. Here are two you can have ready if you need to cover up a mistake.

You will need a table to do your tricks on. Cover it with a cloth if you have one. Before the show, arrange the chairs for the audience. Make sure everyone sits in front of the table and not too close to it. If you can, put a dim light near the front of the table and just to one side.

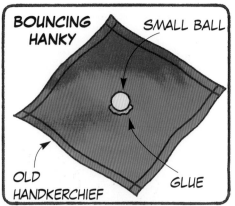

Glue a ball to the middle of a handkerchief. Pull out the hanky and pretend to drop it on the floor. It will bounce back up to your hand.

Cut a large jagged hole in an old hanky. Pretend to sneeze into it. Hold it up to show how strong your sneeze was.

Doctor, doctor! I've only got 59 seconds to live.   Hold on, I'll be with you in a minute!

Magic boxes

You can use this magic box for making things appear or disapppear – by magic!

YOU WILL NEED

- a shoe box or box with lid

- a piece of cardboard the same size as the lid and a piece the same size as the end of the box.

- a piece of black cardboard, the same length as the box and about 5cm (2in) wider

- 2 rubber bands

- 4 paper fasteners

- paints, sticky tape and scissors

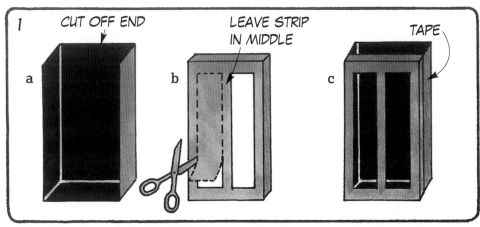

Cut one end off the box (a). Paint the inside black. Cut two long strips out of the lid, leaving a strip down the middle (b).

Put the lid on the box. Stick it down all the way around the edges with sticky tape (c).

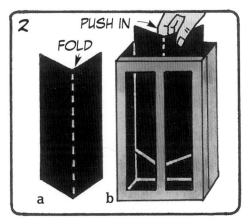

Fold the black cardboard in half, lengthways (a). Push it into the box, like this (b), to make a secret space at the back of the box.

Tape the large piece of cardboard to the side of the box to make a door. Stick the smaller one to the top of the box to make a flap.

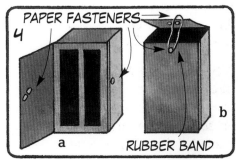

Push paper fasteners through the door and the side of the box (a), the flap and the back of the box (b). Hook a rubber band over the door and side fasteners, and another band over the flap and back fasteners.

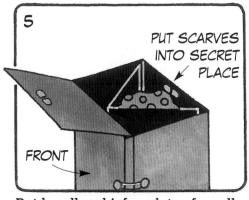

Put handkerchiefs or lots of small flat things into the secret space in the box. Close the door and the flap. Hook up the rubber bands.

Unhook the rubber bands and show people the inside of the box. Put your hand into the space in the front to prove the box is empty.

Close the door and hook up the band. Wave your wand. Open the flap and slowly pull out the things hidden in the back.

What did one eye say to the other eye? Something has come between us that smells!

41

Grand finisher

This is a very good trick to do as the last one in a show. You need a helper in the audience, who pretends he doesn't know what you're going to do. Before you start this trick, ask for a volunteer. Your helper must get up very quickly before anyone else offers.

A few days before the show, find an old shirt for your helper to wear. Write in big letters, with a brush and paint 'The End' across the back of the shirt. Leave the paint to dry.

Ask your helper to sit down. Stand behind him and undo the buttons on his shirt collar and shirt front.

Now undo the buttons on your helper's shirt sleeves.

Take hold of the shirt collar. Say the magic words. Give the shirt a good pull upwards.

Pull the shirt again. Keep on pulling and it will come right off from under the helper's coat.

Turn the shirt around to show what's written on the back. Everyone will clap while you bow.

THE SECRET

Before the show, put the shirt around your helper, so that it hangs down his back. Do not put his arms into the shirt sleeves.

Do up the collar button and the top two front buttons. Put the sleeves down his arms and do up the buttons.

Put on the helper's coat and do up the buttons. Make sure that the shirt looks as if it's on properly and that the sleeves show.

What is black and white and red all over?

A sun burned penguin.

42

Paper Fun

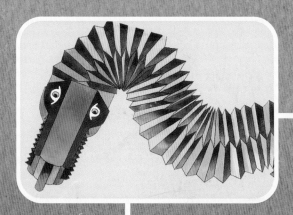

Paper tricks

1 MAGIC LADDER

TAPE

Lay out two sheets of newspaper and roll them up and tape them together, like this.

2

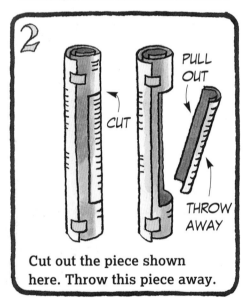

CUT

PULL OUT

THROW AWAY

Cut out the piece shown here. Throw this piece away.

3

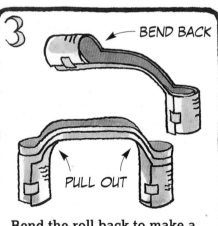

BEND BACK

PULL OUT

Bend the roll back to make a bridge shape. Gently pull out the insides from each side. Here comes the ladder!

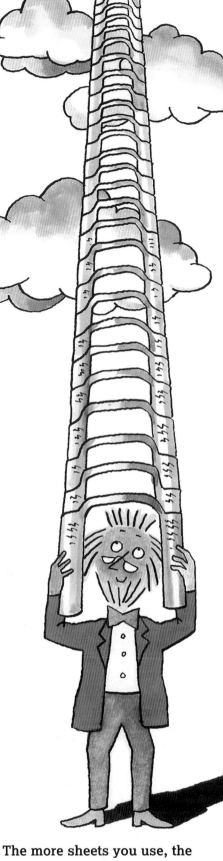

The more sheets you use, the higher your ladder will go. It could go as high as a house! But you'll need strong hands to cut through so much paper.

SURPRISE TRICKS

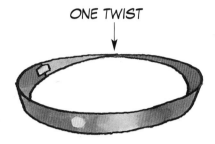

ONE TWIST

Twist a scrap of paper and tape it into a loop. Mark a spot on the paper. Run your finger around and around the loop. Which is the inside of the loop?

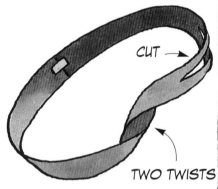

CUT

TWO TWISTS

Now make a loop with two twists. Cut as shown here to make two loops. Surprised?

Q: If you got lost in a blizzard with the Sunday papers, what would you do?

A: Cover your head and stuff your clothes with newspaper. Layers of newspaper trap the air warmed by your body. (This is a real survival trick.)

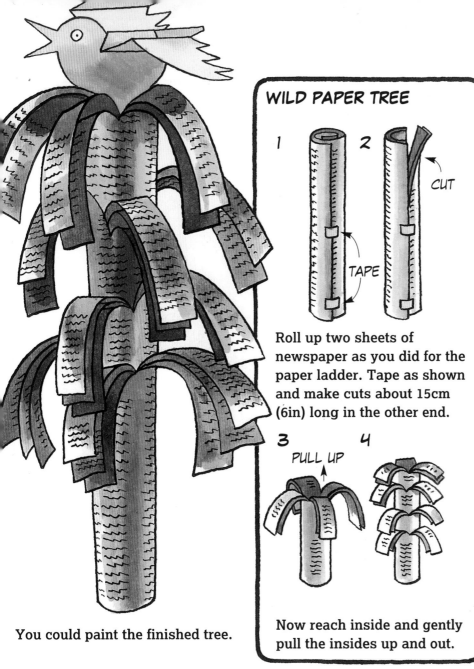

You could paint the finished tree.

WILD PAPER TREE

1 2 → CUT

TAPE

Roll up two sheets of newspaper as you did for the paper ladder. Tape as shown and make cuts about 15cm (6in) long in the other end.

3 PULL UP 4

Now reach inside and gently pull the insides up and out.

1 SITTING BIRD

← SAME SIZE →

Draw a long-legged bird on thick paper and cut it out. Fold some paper and make a wing to fit the bird's back.

2

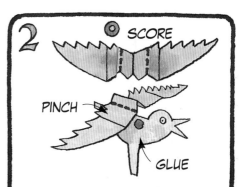

SCORE

PINCH →

GLUE

Unfold the wing and score as shown. Fold each side towards the middle. Dab glue on the back, pinch on the wing and poke the leg into the tree.

WALK THROUGH POSTCARD

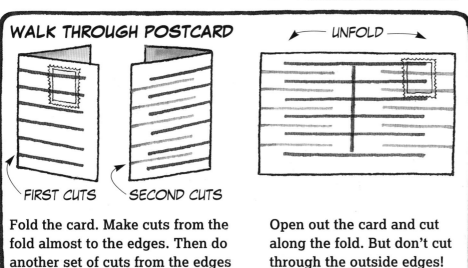

← UNFOLD →

FIRST CUTS   SECOND CUTS

Fold the card. Make cuts from the fold almost to the edges. Then do another set of cuts from the edges almost to the fold. Don't cut through!

Open out the card and cut along the fold. But don't cut through the outside edges! Tug and see what happens.

HOW TO SCORE

To score a straight line run the tip of your scissors along the paper against a ruler. Score curved lines without a ruler. Hold the paper firmly.

45

Paper people

KNOW-HOW CIRCLE-MAKER

3CM (1IN) 6CM (2IN) 9CM (3IN)

Measure and poke holes in a strip of cardboard. Stick pencils in the holes. Hold one pencil firm and swing the other around to draw a circle.

HATS WITH BRIMS

— CUT
— SCORE

FOLD OUT

PINCH

ROLL SIDES

Fold a long strip of paper around and glue it together to make a head. Trace around the head and score this mark. Then draw a larger circle and cut it out. Make cuts from the middle to the scored line. Push the head through the middle. Glue a strip around the top. You can pinch the front or roll sides to make different brims.

FACES

Glue on a cone nose, or cut and fold the shape shown above.

SCORE

Glue big circles for eyes, or roll a tiny strip and glue before sticking on. Add eyelashes and moustache.

CONE HATS

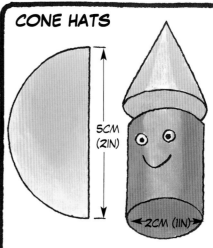

5CM (2IN)

2CM (1IN)

Use the circle-maker to make a semi-circle at least 2½ times as big across as the head. Roll it into a cone and glue.

CUT

COTTON WOOL BALLS

For a Santa hat, glue on cotton wool. For a Robin Hood hat, slice off the top. Make cuts in a feather shape and glue it on.

HAIR

SCORE

Cut and score a strip of thick paper as shown above. Curl the bottom strips carefully with scissors, to make curly hair. Dab glue inside the head, fold over the hair and stick it down.

For finger puppets, make tubes that fit your fingers.

Haunted house

Because of the way your eye works, paper figures can look mysteriously large and real when you squint at them through a peep-hole. Attach some of the figures to threads and pull-tabs and you can make a tiny stage inside the box.

YOU WILL NEED

- a shoe box
- tissue paper
- thick paper
- ruler and scissors
- needle and thread
- glue and paints

HOW TO CUT PANELS

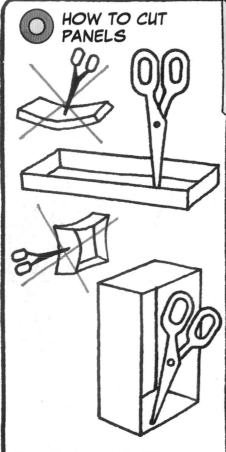

Turn the box so that the side you want to cut lies flat against something hard. Carefully poke a hole with the tip of the scissors.

FIX THE LID

CUT

COVER

DAB GLUE

Cut panels in the lid. Dab on glue and lay a piece of tissue paper on top. Cut out small bats and spiders from thick paper. Take a needle and knotted thread, push it through a bat and then through the lid. Make a loop with the other end of the thread so you can dangle it.

1 FIX THE BOX

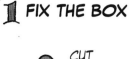

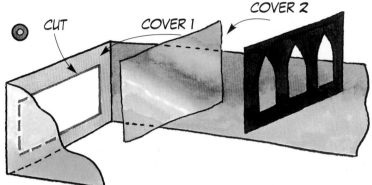

CUT

COVER 1

COVER 2

Cut a panel from the back of the box. Turn it into a special window by covering it first with tissue paper (1), then with cut-out paper (2). Now paint the walls and floor.

2

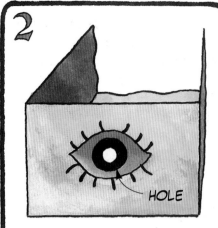

HOLE

Make a small hole in the front and paint a spooky eye around it.

3

TAB

FEET TABS

Make stand-out figures and scenery with tabs on one side. Glue the tabs to the side of the box. Make figures with tabs at the base to stand up in the middle of the box. They must all face forwards, tabs towards the back.

ACTION FIGURE - RISING SKELETON

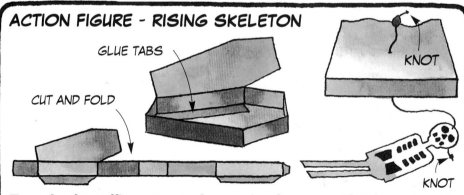

GLUE TABS

CUT AND FOLD

KNOT

KNOT

To make the coffin, cut out a long strip of paper, with tabs and a lid, like this. Bend it around, glue the sides of the coffin together and glue the tabs to the box. Then make a skeleton. Use needle and thread to make a cord that goes through the skeleton and the lid, like this. Pull it and the skeleton rises – let go and the skeleton drops.

ACTION FIGURE - PROWLING MONSTER

PAPER SLIDE

Cut slots in the box and make a long slide of thick paper. Glue a figure to it. Glue paper stops at the ends. You can push the slide back and forth.

Paper zoo

To make a stand-up animal, just cut the shape with its back along the fold of a piece of paper. Then you can curl, glue and fold to make bending necks, curling tails and 3D ears and wings. You will find patterns for more animals on pages 52-53. For how to score, see page 45.

YOU WILL NEED

- thick paper
- scissors and glue
- bright paints or pens to decorate

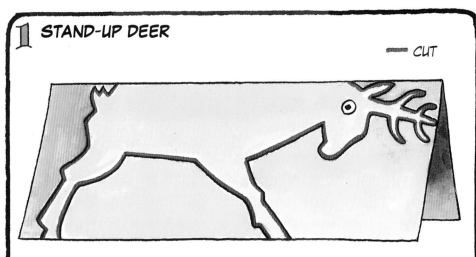

1 STAND-UP DEER

——— CUT

Fold the paper in half and draw the deer with his back and neck along the fold. Then cut around the outline through both layers of paper.

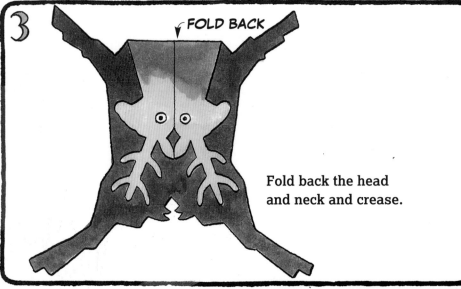

3 FOLD BACK

Fold back the head and neck and crease.

4

PUSH DOWN

PUSH BACK

Push the fold down and push the neck back as shown.

2

— SCORE

Open flat and score as shown here.

Paper zoo patterns

PIGLET

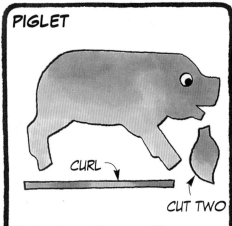

CURL

CUT TWO

Cut out ear shapes with a small tab. Curl the ears and tail before gluing them on.

MOUSE

PUSH DOWN

FOLD BACK

— SCORE

Fold and score a mouse cut-out as shown. Push down and back so that the mouse's head is tucked between its shoulders. Add a long curling tail. Hang it by the tail.

LION AND TIGER

CURL

CUT TWO

For the lion's mane, cut a deep fringe in a strip of paper. Curl the fringe. Fold and glue on the neck.

FLAPPING DUCK

— SCORE

Score and fold the wing and glue it to the duck. If the duck leans forward, put a tiny piece of poster tack behind its tail.

SEAL

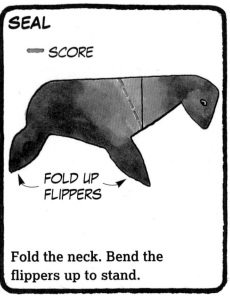

— SCORE

FOLD UP FLIPPERS

Fold the neck. Bend the flippers up to stand.

SNAKE

Curl a short way, then turn to curl another bit. Continue like this to make a ripply body for the snake.

GIRAFFE

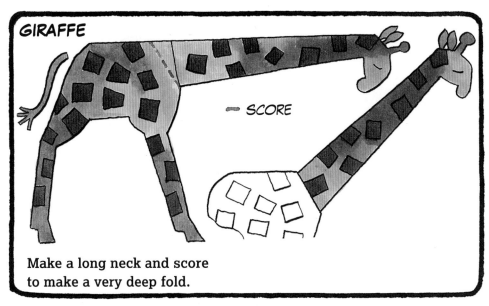

— SCORE

Make a long neck and score to make a very deep fold.

DUCK AND CHICKEN

— SCORE

Fold over a wing shape, fringed as shown.

COW AND ELEPHANT

CUT TWO

CURL

Curl tusks before gluing them on.

PONY

— CUT
— SCORE

GLUE MANE

Make a neck fold in the same way you did for the deer on page 50. Then cut along the neck and glue a fringed mane between the neck halves. Add a tail the same way. To lower the head, just push down the neck and crease again.

ZEBRA

— CUT
— SCORE

The zebra is like the pony.

Paper flowers

The stretchiness of crêpe paper is very useful. You can pull it into petal shapes or ruffled edges. With tissue paper you can show the vein of a leaf by making a lengthwise crease.

YOU WILL NEED

- crêpe paper
- tissue paper
- sticky tape and scissors
- strong glue with a nozzle
- thin sticks or light wire (such as satay or kebab sticks or florist's wire) for the stems.

DAISIES

CALYX – THE PART BEHIND A FLOWER HEAD

MIDDLE

Cut petals around a circle. Sandwich petals and stem between a middle circle and calyx shape and glue together.

1 CRÊPE PAPER POPPIES

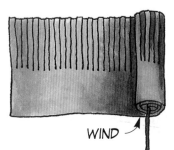

WIND

For the middle, make lots of cuts in a strip of paper, like this. Glue one end of the strip to the stem, wind it around and around, and glue it together.

2

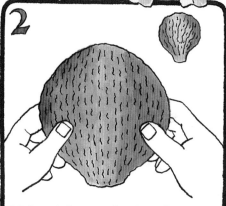

Make eight petals. Cut them with the grain of the paper running up and down. Shape them by stretching sideways.

3

OVERLAP

FOLD END OF LEAF

Glue the petals around the stem. Then glue a long strip of paper under the flower and wind it down the stem, gluing in leaf shapes as you do so.

1 TISSUE PAPER ROSES

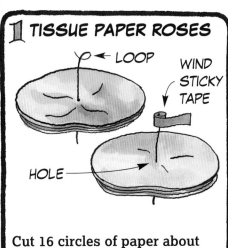

Cut 16 circles of paper about 16cm (6in) across. Make a wire stem as shown.

2

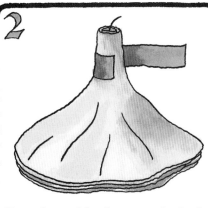

Turn it upside-down and pinch the flower tightly around the stem as shown. Bind into a shape with sticky tape.

3

CALYX

Cut out a calyx. Slide it down the stem and glue it to the flower.

4

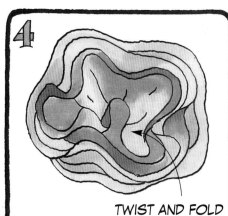

TWIST AND FOLD

Turn the flower up again and shape it by pulling the petals out as shown.

CARNATIONS

1

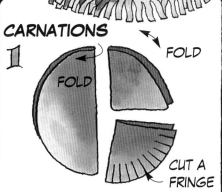

FOLD

FOLD

CUT A FRINGE

Cut 13 circles of thin paper, about 9cm (3in) across. Fold each into a quarter-circle. Make cuts, like this.

2

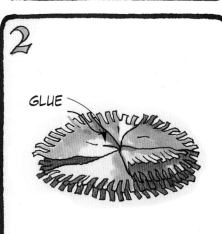

GLUE

Open the circle flat. Glue the quarter-circles onto it in layers.

3

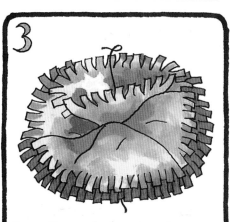

Loop the end of some wire and push it through to make a stem. Glue a strip of green paper around the stem.

Crocodile marionette (1)

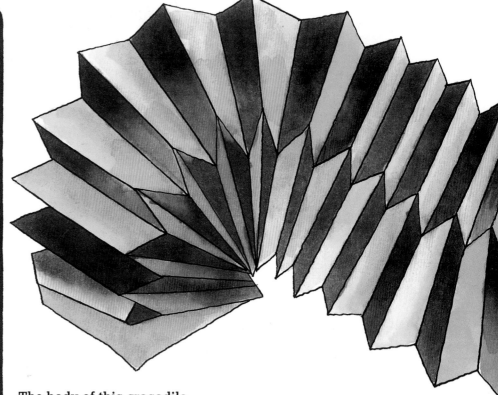

PAPER SPRING

1

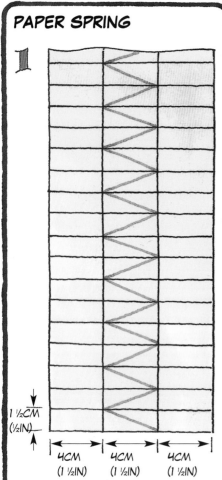

1 ½CM (½IN)

4CM (1 ½IN) 4CM (1 ½IN) 4CM (1 ½IN)

Use paper 12cm (5in) wide and as long as possible. If you glue strips together, let the glue dry before you do the next step. Rule lines as shown in black and make a zig-zag (shown in green).

The body of this crocodile marionette is made from a strip of paper folded into a special spring. This makes a shape that can bend and twist and wriggle when you move the hanging strings. The fold is tricky until you get the hang of it, so follow the instructions carefully.

YOU WILL NEED

- yellow or green paper
- ruler and scissors
- glue and string
- bright pencils or felt-tip pens
- 2 small sticks or rods

Turn the page to see how to make the head of the crocodile and how to work the strings.

2

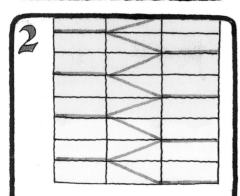

Now make more lines (shown in green) joining the points of the zig-zag to the edges. Score all the green lines and crease them firmly.

3

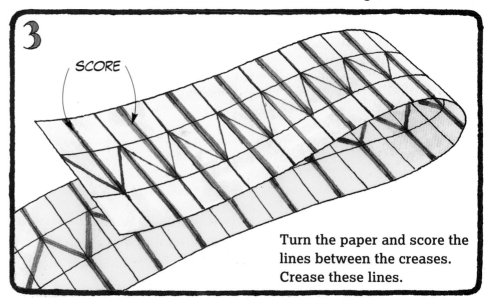

SCORE

Turn the paper and score the lines between the creases. Crease these lines.

4 Hold the paper as shown. Walk your thumbs along the sides to push the creases inwards and pinch the folds between your fingers.

5 Continue until all the folds can be pinched between your fingers to make a shape like this.

57

Crocodile marionette (2)

1 MAKE THE CROC

— CUT

Take some paper about 40 x 10cm (16 x 4in) and fold it in half. Draw and cut out the head shape.

2

SCORE

GLUE TEETH

GLUE TONGUE

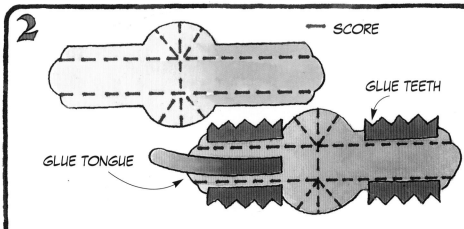

Open and score the head shape as shown. Turn the head and glue strips of paper teeth inside the jaw.

Glue the end of a long tongue to the back of the top jaw.

3

PUSH IN

Now fold all the scored lines inward. Push in the crease between the V-shaped score at each side of the jaw.

4

GLUE

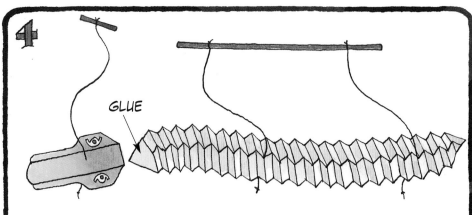

Glue the paper spring to the back of the head. String up the crocodile with a needle and knotted thread as shown.

Tie the head string to a small stick. Tie the two back strings to another stick.

WORK THE CROC

Raise the head string to make the crocodile rear up. Jerk the string to make its jaws open and close.

Rock the stick back and forth to make the crocodile hump its back as it moves along.

Hold your arms like this to make the crocodile turn and chase its tail.

Experiments

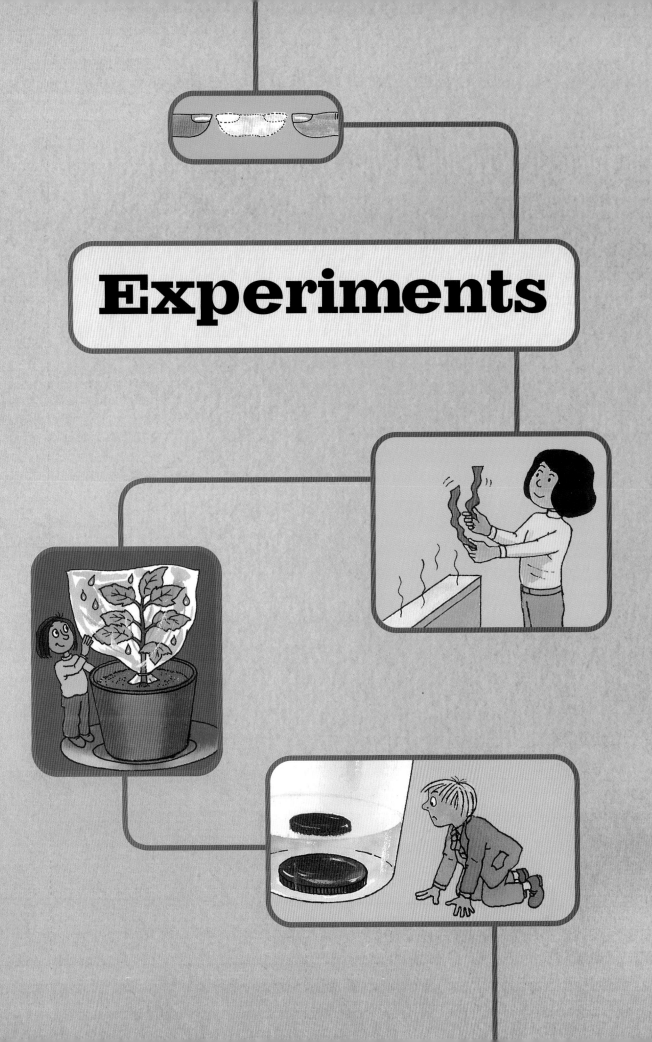

Can you believe your eyes?

If you can see something, then you know it is real – unless it is magic, of course. Here are a few ways to test whether your eyes are telling you the truth or if they sometimes deceive you. Try these tricks yourself and then ask other people to do them. You will need a ruler to check the answers. You may be in for a few surprises. Keep a score of the ones you get right.

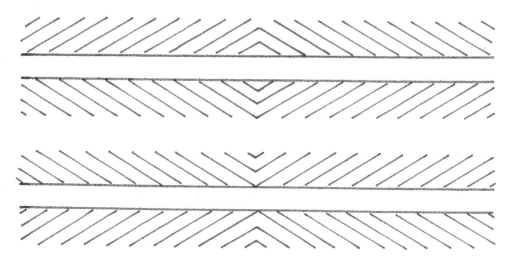

Are all the green lines straight or do they bend a little? Do the top ones get wider at each end? Do the underneath ones get wider in the middle? To find out, put the edge of a ruler along each green line.

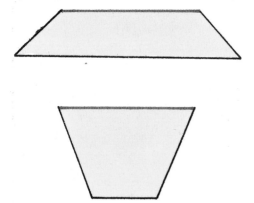

Look at these two shapes. Is the top red line longer than the lower red line? Measure them with a ruler to find the answer.

USE A RULER TO MEASURE ALL THE LINES.

Are these two red lines the same length? Use a ruler to find out.

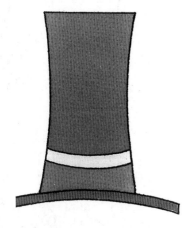

This is a funny hat but is it as high as the brim is wide?

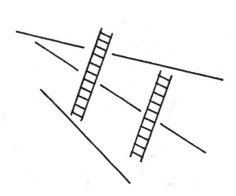

Which of these two ladders is the longer one; or are they both the same length?

WHY IT WORKS

When we look at things, our brains are sometimes fooled. These things are called optical illusions, which means we see things which are not really true.

When you look at the green lines at the top of this page, your eyes are misled by the red lines, so the green lines look bent. It is the same with all the other tricks. When you measure them with a ruler, you find all the lines are the same length. How many did you get right?

Here are some more tricks to play with your eyes. Try them yourself first. Then tell other people how to do them but don't tell them what they'll see so they get a surprise. You can always pretend it is a bit of magic that only you can do.

For the Hole in Your Hand trick you need a paper or cardboard tube. You can make one out of a piece of paper.

HOW MANY FINGERS?

Hold one finger of each hand up in front of your eyes, about 20cm (8in) away from your face. Stare at something beyond your fingers, not at them.

YOU WILL SEE

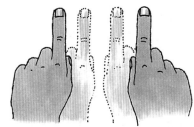

If you stare hard, you will see three or four ghostly fingers in front of your eyes. Look at your two fingers and the other two will disappear.

FLOATING FINGER

STARE HARD JUST BEYOND YOUR FINGERS.

Hold one finger of each hand up in front of your eyes, like this. Stare hard between them.

YOU WILL SEE

If you stare hard at the gap between your fingers, you will see a short finger appear between them. The odd thing about it is that it has a nail on each end.

WHY IT WORKS

You see four fingers in the How Many Fingers? trick because you are looking beyond your fingers. So you see two fingers with each eye, making four in all. With the Floating Finger trick, the two extra fingers overlap to make an extra finger in the middle. You see a hole in your hand because one eye is looking down the tube and the other is looking at your hand. These two views mix together so you see a hand with a hole in it. They all work because you have two eyes.

HOLE IN YOUR HAND

LOOK DOWN THE TUBE AND KEEP THE OTHER EYE OPEN.

Hold a tube up to your right eye. Hold your left hand up beside the tube, like this. Stare very hard down the tube.

MAKING A TUBE

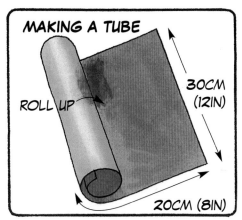

ROLL UP

30CM (12IN)

20CM (8IN)

Make a tube by rolling up a sheet of thick paper, about 30 x 20cm (12 x 8in). Stick the edge down with sticky tape or glue.

YOU WILL SEE

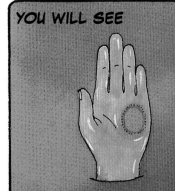

Stare hard down the tube with your right eye, keeping your left eye open. You can see your hand and then you will see a hole you can look through.

Seeing the invisible

You can't see noises – even nice ones like music or unpleasant ones like the screeching of car brakes – but you hear them all the time. There is always noise of some sort and, if you listen hard, you can always hear something. Here are two ways to find out about noise.

YOU WILL NEED

- a thin plastic bag
- a big tin or bowl, a spoon and a baking tray
- a rubber band and paper
- kitchen foil and thread
- a glass

BANG THE TRAY AS HARD AS YOU CAN. WATCH THE SUGAR JUMP!

1 JUMPING PAPER

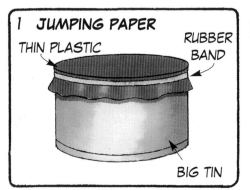

THIN PLASTIC
RUBBER BAND
BIG TIN

Cut along one side and the bottom of a plastic bag. Spread it tightly over the top of a big tin or bowl. Stretch a rubber band around the tin or bowl to make a drum.

2

PIECES OF PAPER

Tear up some paper into very small pieces. Put them on top of the drum. Tap the drum with a spoon, and the paper will jump.

3 JUMPING SUGAR

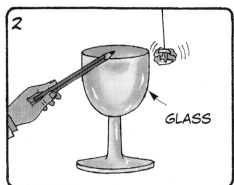

BAKING TRAY
SUGAR

Sprinkle some sugar on top of the drum. Hold the baking tray close to the drum. Hit the tray hard with a big spoon. Watch carefully and you will see the sugar jump.

1 JUMPING BALL

THREAD
TAPE
KITCHEN FOIL

Put a glass down on a table. Scrunch a small piece of kitchen foil into a ball. Cut a piece of thread, about 30cm (12in) long, and stick it to it with tape.

2

GLASS

Hold up the thread so the foil ball just hangs against the edge of the glass, like this. Tap the glass gently with a pencil and the ball will jump away.

WHY IT WORKS

When you hit the drum, tray or glass, they all waggle when they make a noise. This is called vibration and makes the paper, sugar and foil jump around. When anything vibrates it makes the air around it vibrate. The air then carries the vibration to your ears so you hear a noise.

You can sometimes feel sound. If you put your hand lightly on a stereo which is on very loud, you can feel it vibrating.

High and low notes

When you play a tune on a musical instrument, you have to make different notes. If the instrument has strings, you press them with your fingers. If it is an instrument you blow, you put your fingers over the holes to play a tune. Here are two ways to find out about music – even if you cannot play anything.

BIG INSTRUMENTS MAKE LOW NOTES. LITTLE ONES MAKE HIGH NOTES.

YOU WILL NEED

- a ruler
- a rubber band
- two pencils

1 NOISY RULER

PULL DOWN AND LET GO

Put a ruler on a table, with most of it over the edge, like this. Hold the part on the table down with a book. Pull the other end down and let it go. It makes a low twang.

2

PULL DOWN AND LET GO

Push the ruler further in under the book and pull it down again. It makes a higher twang. Push it in a bit more and the noise gets higher. You can see the ruler waggling.

1 RULER GUITAR

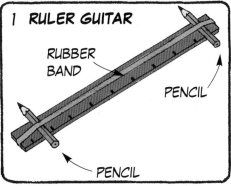

RUBBER BAND

PENCIL

PENCIL

Stretch a long rubber band over a ruler, like this. Push a pencil under the band at one end and a second pencil under the band at the other end.

WHY IT WORKS

LOW NOISE   HIGH NOISE

When a ruler or band is long, it vibrates slowly and makes a low noise. When it is short, it vibrates quickly and makes high noises. High and low sounds depend on how fast things vibrate.

2

SLIDE PENCIL ALONG

Pluck the band with one finger. Push one pencil along the ruler a bit and pluck the band again. It will make a higher note. You can play a tune – very slowly.

DID YOU KNOW?

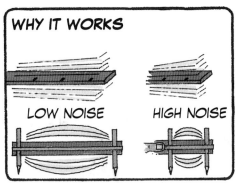

Players of string instruments press the strings to shorten them and make higher notes. They tighten or loosen the strings before they play. Tight strings vibrate more quickly and make higher notes.

Light tricks

All light – light from the Sun, from electric light and from fires – usually travels in straight lines. If it could go around corners, there would be no shadows when the Sun shines, or shadows in a room. But light does strange things when it goes through the air and then through water. Here are some ways to find out what it does.

YOU WILL NEED

- a glass of water and a straw or a pencil
- a bowl of water and a coin

THE STRAW LOOKS QUITE STRAIGHT FROM HERE.

Put a straw or a pencil into a glass of water. Hold the glass up level with your eyes and the straw or pencil will look broken.

1 MAGIC COIN

DROP IN COIN

Drop a small coin into a bowl. Tilt the bowl until you cannot see the coin over the edge.

2

WATER

Hold the bowl in exactly the same position so you still can't quite see the coin. Pour water slowly into the bowl and the coin will gradually reappear.

MOVING COIN

MOVE UP AND DOWN

Now hold the bowl up so you can see the coin. Move the bowl slowly up and down, staring at the coin. As you watch, it seems to move up and down in the bowl.

WHY IT WORKS

Light going through air, and then through water at an angle, bends as it goes into water and out again. This makes the straw look broken and the coin reappear in the bowl.

DID YOU KNOW?

If you don't know about light and water you might find it hard to catch a fish. The fish will look higher up in the water than it really is. This is because the light beams you see have been bent by the water. The river will also look much shallower than it is.

When you look down at a pool of still water you can see your own face in it. The water acts like a mirror. Before people knew how to make mirrors, they used bowls of water instead. If you could look up from underneath the water, the top of it would also act like a mirror. Try these ways of finding out about water.

I CAN SEE ONLY ONE COIN. HOW MANY CAN YOU SEE?

YOU WILL NEED

- a glass, water and a coin
- a square glass or clear plastic container
- water and a teaspoon of milk
- a piece of paper and a book
- a flashlight

ONE OR TWO COINS?

Drop a coin in a glass with about 2cm (1in) of water in it. Hold the glass up in front of your eyes. You will see a big coin on the bottom and a small one just above it.

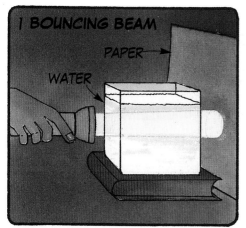

1 BOUNCING BEAM
PAPER
WATER

Stand a square container, full of water, on a book. Prop up a piece of paper at one end. Draw the curtains or switch off the light. Shine a flashlight like this.

2
PAPER
WATER

If you shine the light straight through, the beam comes out in a straight line. If you shine the light at an angle, the beam comes out at an angle on the paper.

3
MILK

To see the beam more clearly, stir a teaspoon of milk into the water. Then try shining the light through the water from lots of different angles to see how the beam bends.

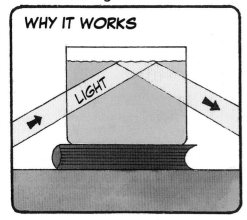

WHY IT WORKS

LIGHT

When light shines straight into water, it goes in a straight line. When a beam hits the top of the water at an angle, it is bounced back at an angle by the water.

DID YOU KNOW?

LAYER OF WARM AIR
SUNLIGHT
LAYER OF HOT AIR

On a very hot day, you sometimes see puddles on a road, but they vanish when you get near. These are called mirages and they're seen in deserts. In this picture light from the sky is bent by a layer of hot air on the ground. So, the man sees a reflection of sky and clouds on the ground, which looks like pools of blue water.

65

What makes a rainbow?

Look for rainbows in the sky when the Sun is shining and it is raining at the same time. You can also see rainbows in the spray from garden hoses, fountains and waterfalls. But to see rainbows, you have to stand with your back to the Sun, facing the raindrops.

HOW TO MAKE A RAINBOW

MIRROR
WATER
BOWL

You will have to do this on a sunny day. Fill a small bowl with water. Put a small mirror into the bowl so that the Sun shines on it.

Hold up a piece of white paper as still as you can, so the Sun shining on the mirror reflects onto the paper.

WHY IT WORKS

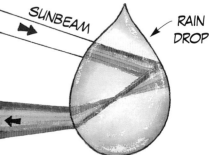

SUNBEAM
RAIN DROP

When sunlight goes through a water drop, the light is split up and creates a rainbow.

RAINBOWS IN GLASS

White light shining through glass with sharp angles in it is split up into a rainbow. You can see some rainbows in precious stones, like diamonds, and in cut glass. The best shape of glass for making rainbows is one like a tent, called a prism.

DID YOU KNOW?

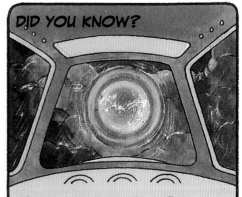

If you were in a plane flying towards a rain storm, with the Sun behind you, you would see a circular moving rainbow.

66

Fill in a circle of cardboard with bright paint or felt-tip pens to look like this. Spin it very fast to see how it can change.

WATCH WHAT HAPPENS...

DRAW AROUND

Put a cup down on a piece of cardboard and draw around it. Cut around the line with scissors to make a neat circle.

2

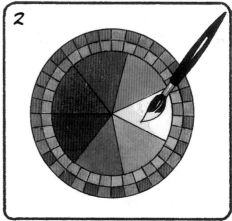

A rainbow is made up of red, orange, yellow, green, blue, indigo and violet. There are lots of shades in between them.

You can paint the spinner just red, yellow, green and blue, if you like. The squares on the outside of this spinner blur into the other sections.

Draw six lines from the middle of the circle to the outside edge to make seven sections. Paint each section in rainbow shades.

WHY IT WORKS

When the spinner goes very fast, our eyes see the different shades but they get mixed up in our brains. Our brains tell us the spinner looks a murky white.

3

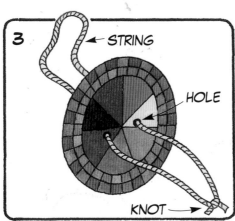

STRING

HOLE

KNOT

Make two holes in the circle, about 1cm (½ in) apart, like this. Thread the ends of a long piece of string through the holes. Tie the ends in a knot.

4

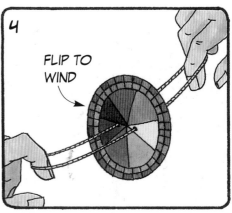

FLIP TO WIND

Hold the loops of string like this. Flip the circle around to twist up the string. Pull your hands apart and then let the string go slack. This will make the circle spin fast.

67

What makes a thunderstorm?

The different kinds of clouds you see in the sky mean that different kinds of weather are coming. When you see huge, tall clouds, like puffy castles, they may mean a thunderstorm is on its way, with flashes of lightning.

A flash is a huge, hot electric spark. You can make a little one safely at home, but it may make your fingers prick and tingle a bit.

THOSE BIG CLOUDS MAY MEAN A THUNDERSTORM IS COMING.

1 MAKING A SPARK

POSTER TACK

BAKING TRAY

Press a large lump of poster tack onto the middle of a very big baking tray or small tin tray. Press it hard so it sticks well.

2

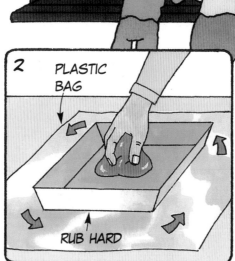

PLASTIC BAG

RUB HARD

Put the tray down on a very large, thick plastic bag. Hold the poster tack lump and rub the tray around and around on the bag.

3

LIFT UP TRAY

TIN LID

Turn off the light and pick up the tray by the poster tack. Hold something metal, such as a tin lid, close to one corner. You may see a spark jump from the tray to the tin.

WHY IT WORKS

When you rub the tray on the bag, it makes electricity, called static electricity. When there is enough static, there is a spark. Static electricity builds up in clouds before a thunderstorm.

DID YOU KNOW?

Most lightning flashes jump from one cloud to another. A few strike the earth and may do damage. Tall buildings have lightning conductors to carry the electricity safely down into the ground. The thunder you hear after a flash is made by lightning. The spark heats the air around it and the air expands very quickly. This sets off a giant wave of air which makes the thunder you hear.

Why is a sunset red?

When the Sun first rises in the morning, the sky often looks red, especially if there are a few clouds about. During the day, when the Sun is overhead, the Sun looks yellow and the sky looks blue. When the Sun sets, it may turn a fiery red and the sky may turn pink.

Do they really change or do they just look as if they do? Here is a way to find out.

THE SUN IS BRIGHT RED NOW IT IS SO LOW ON THE SEA.

1 Fill a clean glass jar with cold water. Stir in one teaspoonful of milk. Hold a flashlight to the side of the jar, like this, in a dark room. The water looks blue.

2 Now move the light around so it is shining through the jar at you, like this. The light looks yellow, like the Sun during the day.

3 Stir in two more teaspoonfuls of milk. Hold the light to the side of the jar. The water still looks blue. Hold it so it shines at you, and the water looks pink.

MILK AND WATER

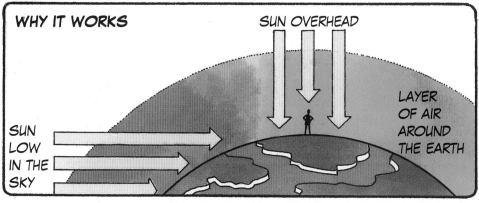

WHY IT WORKS

SUN OVERHEAD

LAYER OF AIR AROUND THE EARTH

SUN LOW IN THE SKY

The Earth is wrapped up in a blanket of air which is full of bits of dust and water drops too small to see. The dust and water drops, like the milk in the glass of water, scatter the blue part of sunlight to make the sky look blue. When the Sun is low in the sky, it looks red because its light has to go further through the air, and only the red part of it comes through to your eyes.

DID YOU KNOW?

If you looked out of a window of a spacecraft, the sky would look black and you would see stars in the day. This is because there is no dusty air in space to break up white light into a blue sky or a sunset.

69

Rubbing and warming

Have you ever noticed that things get warm when you rub them? On cold days, people rub their hands together or rub their hands on their sleeves to warm them. Try it and your hands will soon warm up. There are lots of things which get warm and even very hot when they are rubbed. Here are a few for you to try. There are lots more you can probably think of yourself.

RUB HARD AND THEN FEEL HOW WARM IT IS.

Try rubbing two dry sticks or pieces of wood together as hard as you can. After about 20 rubs, feel the wood. It will be quite warm.

Rub two pieces of metal, such as tin lids, together. Rub a piece of wood and sandpaper. After a minute or so, they will be quite hot.

When you ride a bicycle and brake hard, the brake blocks rub on the wheel to slow you down. Try braking while riding quite slowly. Then feel the brake blocks.

Scuff your shoes hard across the floor. Then feel the bottoms of your shoes. Try rubbing your bare foot hard on a carpet. It will soon feel quite warm.

WHY IT WORKS

Like most things, your hands, wood and metal all have rough surfaces. You can see this if you look at them closely or with a magnifying glass. When they move against each other, the roughness slows down the movement. This is called friction. The rougher two things are, the harder you have to work to move them. The work is turned into heat and the things become hot.

DID YOU KNOW?

Car wheels warm up because of the friction between them and the road. After a long journey, they may be too hot to touch. This warms the road too. Ice on roads melts if lots of cars go over it.

When a spacecraft returns to Earth, friction between it and the air makes it very hot. Its special shape and shield of special materials stop people inside from being burned up.

Slipping and gripping

Rough surfaces are useful because they grip together and stop slipping. Your shoes grip a slippery floor. Bicycle brake blocks are made of a special material to grip the wheel rim. Car wheels have ridges in them to help grip the road.

But this grip is a nuisance when we want things to slide easily. Slippery oil is poured into machines so the moving parts slide over each other. Here are some ways to make things slip around easily.

SHOES WITH SMOOTH SOLES SLIDE MORE EASILY THAN ROUGH SOLES.

The rough soles of your shoes stop you from slipping. You slide on ice because the pressure of your shoes melts the ice a little. You slide on a very thin sheet of water which then freezes again.

1
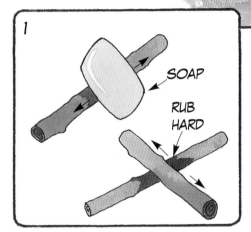

SOAP
RUB HARD

Find two dry sticks or pieces of wood. Rub a piece of soap over one of them. Now rub the sticks together. They will slide over each other and stay cool.

2

WOOD
WATER

Put a small block of wood on a table. Give it a knock to make it slide. Now pour a little soapy water on the table. Knock the block again to see what happens.

3
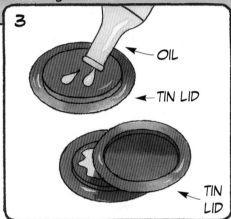

OIL
TIN LID
TIN LID

Pour a little oil on a flat tin lid. Any oil, such as cooking oil, will do. Rub the lid with another lid. You can feel the lids slide over each other on the oil.

WHY IT WORKS
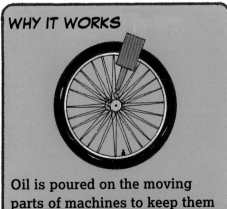

Oil is poured on the moving parts of machines to keep them slightly apart. They slide over each other on a layer of oil without touching, and don't get hot. This is called lubrication.

DID YOU KNOW?

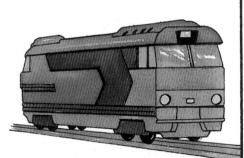

Cars skid on greasy, wet or icy roads because grease, water and ice make a layer between the wheels and the road. The wheels cannot grip so the car skids.

All machines with parts which slide over each other need oil or grease lubrication. Without it, they would rub and could get so hot they would melt.

Ups and downs of plants

If you plant a seed upside down, does it grow upside down? Or does it turn itself around and grow the right way? Try growing some beans or peas to find out what happens to the roots and stems.

YOU WILL NEED

- 6 beans or peas (the kind sold for growing, not for eating)
- some soil (the sort sold in bags called potting compost is best)
- a pot or bowl
- a little plastic bottle
- black paper, a rubber band and scissors

1 WATER / SOIL

Fill the bowl or pot with soil or compost. Press it down with your fingers. Fill the bowl with water and wait until it has sunk into the soil.

2 PRESS IN BEANS

Press the beans or peas into the soil. Put the bowl in a warm, light place and wait for the seeds to sprout. They will take about a week to split and grow.

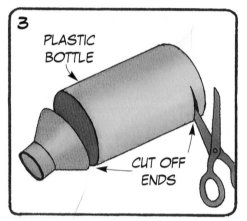

3 PLASTIC BOTTLE / CUT OFF ENDS

When the seeds have sprouted, cut the top and bottom off a small plastic bottle. It should be big enough to slip a bean or pea in easily with room to spare.

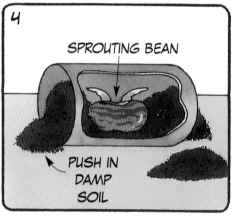

4 SPROUTING BEAN / PUSH IN DAMP SOIL

Push one bean or pea into the bottle. Push damp soil in at each end. Pack it well around the seed. Drip on a little water at each end.

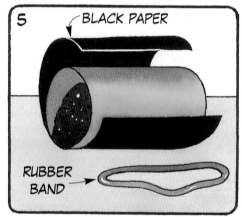

5 BLACK PAPER / RUBBER BAND

Wrap a piece of black paper around the bottle, leaving the ends open. Put the bottle in a warm, light place. Look at it every day.

TURN THE BOTTLE FOR A DAY AND THE SHOOTS WILL GROW THE OTHER WAY.

When two shoots come out of the bottle, one grows up and has tiny green leaves. The other, the white root, grows down. Turn the bottle over for a day and a night. The shoots will grow the other way.

WHY IT WORKS

Whichever way you plant seeds, the stems will always grow up to the light. The roots always grow down into the earth in search of water and food.

72

All plants need water to keep alive and to grow. They get the water through their roots and it goes up their stems. Plants also give out water through their leaves in such tiny drops you cannot see them. Try these experiments with plants.

YOU WILL NEED

- a stick of fresh celery
- a table knife
- ink or water paint
- a bush or branch of a tree growing outside
- a plastic bag
- a piece of string

1 SUCKING UP WATER

INK OR FOOD DYE

CUT OFF

Slice the end off a stick of celery. Put the stick in a jar with a little water. Pour in a couple of drops of ink or food dye. Stand the jar in a warm, light place for a day.

2

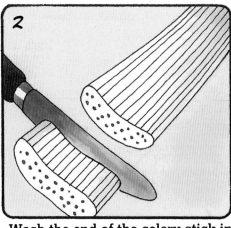

Wash the end of the celery stick in clean water. Slice the stem about every 3cm (1in). Look at each cut. You can see dots where the stem has taken up the inky water.

1 BREATHING OUT WATER

PLASTIC BAG

STRING

Put a plastic bag over a small branch of leaves on a bush or small tree in a sunny place. Tie it on with string, like this. Leave it for two or three days.

2

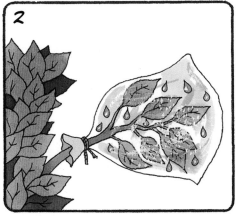

Look at the bag every day and you will see drops of water on the inside of the bag. If the days are very hot, quite a lot of water will collect in the bag.

WHY IT WORKS

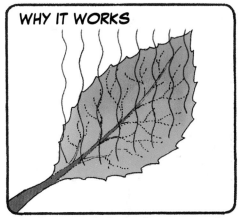

The leaves of plants have very tiny holes all over them. On hot days, tiny drops of water come out from these holes into the air. These collect on the inside of the bag.

DID YOU KNOW?

On a very hot day, a tree, such as a birch or elm, may take up as much as 50 large buckets of water. This comes out invisibly through its leaves into the air.

Try tying a plastic bag around a plant indoors. Water it and stand it on a windowsill in the Sun.

THIS FLOWER IS GREEN FROM JUST A DROP OF INK!

Try putting a white flower stem in bright inky water. The petals will soon show the shade of ink.

Where do clouds come from?

After a shower of rain, all the water on the roads, the grass, the houses and even your clothes, slowly dries up and disappears. The puddles get smaller and smaller until they vanish. The water disappears much more quickly when the weather is hot and sunny. When it is cold and damp, the wet things take much longer to dry. But where does the water go? And where do the rain clouds come from? How does all that water get into the sky to make rain? Here are ways to find out.

ON HOT, SUNNY DAYS, PUDDLES DRY UP VERY QUICKLY.

1 WATER INTO AIR

Put a big plate on a sunny windowsill. Pour some cold water onto the plate. Leave it for three hours. Look at it often and you will see the water disappear.

2

Put two plates in a sunny place. Pour about half a cup of water on to each one. Shade one with a book, like this. Look at them after an hour or two and see what happens.

WHY IT WORKS

When water dries up, it turns into tiny drops, so small you cannot see them. This is called evaporation. The water drops go into the air. This damp air rises. On warm days, it rises all the time, taking tiny droplets of water up to the sky. In the sky it is much cooler than down on the ground. The tiny drops of water join up to make bigger drops. These make the clouds you see in the sky.

WARM AIR GOES UP

Cut a few strips of the thinnest paper you can find. Tissue paper or thin cellophane work well. If you hold them over a radiator or heater, they flutter upwards.

DID YOU KNOW?

On warmer days, the water in clouds falls as rain. It runs into ponds, lakes, rivers and then to the sea. Water from all wet things, even clothes on a washing line, goes up into the air and makes more clouds which may rain again.

Why does it rain?

Try these experiments and find out how water comes from warm damp air.

IT IS RAINING HERE BUT IT IS SNOWING HIGH ON THE MOUNTAINS.

1 WATER FROM THE AIR

COLD PLATE

HOT WATER

Fill a bowl with hot water. Hold a cold plate over the bowl for about a minute. Turn the plate over. It is covered with tiny drops of water.

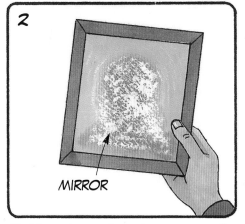

2

MIRROR

Hold a mirror close to your mouth and breathe on it. Or breathe on a window pane on a cold day. Soon the glass clouds up with tiny drops of water.

3

ICE CUBES

SHINY TIN CAN

Find a clean tin can that is shiny on the outside. Fill the tin can with ice cubes. After a few minutes, the outside of the tin will be covered with water drops.

WHY IT WORKS

Warm air has lots of water droplets in it. When it touches something cold, the tiny water drops collect into big drops so you can see them. This is called condensation. When warm air rises up to meet cold air in the sky, the tiny drops of water collect around specks of dust in the air. As more collect, they make a cloud. If there is enough water in low clouds, it falls as rain.

DEW

The water drops you see on grass and leaves on some mornings are water from the air. During the night the ground gets cold and the water in the air collects into drops.

FROST

The white frost you see on a very cold morning on grass or windows is frozen dew. The water which collects on the ground and glass freezes into white ice.

SNOW

When air very high in the sky cools quickly, the water in it freezes into crystals and falls as snow. You can see the snow crystals with a magnifying glass.

Crystal columns

Here is a way to make pillars of soda grow up and down until they meet in the middle. It takes several days to work so you will have to be patient.

YOU WILL NEED

- 2 glass jars
- bicarbonate of soda or baking soda and a spoon
- 4 lengths of wool yarn, each about 35cm (14in) long, twisted together to make a thick string
- hot water from the hot tap
- a large, old plate

Fill two jars with very hot water. Stir in six teaspoons of bicarbonate of soda or baking soda. Continue stirring it in until no more will disappear in the water.

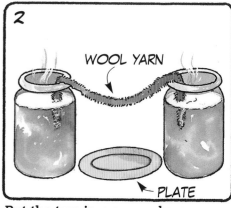

Put the two jars somewhere warm where they will not be moved. Put the plate in between them. Drop the ends of the wool yarn into the jars so the yarn hangs over the plate.

AFTER A FEW DAYS, THE COLUMNS WILL MEET IN THE MIDDLE.

WHY IT WORKS

Water and soda from the jars goes along the wool yarn and drips down. As it drips, the water turns into tiny drops, so small you cannot see them, in the air. The soda is left in a hard drip.

DID YOU KNOW?

The pillars in caves, called stalagmites and stalactites, are made in the same way as the soda column. Water, with lime from limestone rocks, drips from the ceiling. As the water goes into the air, it leaves the lime behind which builds up over hundreds of years, very, very slowly. The stalagmites are the ones growing up from the floor. The stalactites grow down from the ceiling.

Print
& Paint

Before you start

These are the things you need to make the prints in this section:

- Paint – powder or poster paints are good for printing.

- Bright cardboard – use good quality for the best prints. Practise printing on rough paper, such as old wall paper. Some art stores sell pieces of thick, cheap paper called sugar paper.

- Waterproof inks – they're sold in stationery and art stores.

- Fabric dyes – ask in art or craft stores for water-based dyes. You have to buy a fixer for this dye. Read the instructions on the bottles carefully.

- Glitter – you can buy this in tubes or tubs at toy or stationery stores.

- Expanded polystyrene – this white, light plastic stuff is often used for packing breakable things. Try asking for some in a shop or store. Use thick pieces for printing blocks.

- Sponge cloths – used for cleaning. Use it to dab on paint to make sponge rollers.

- Paste – for paint and paste prints, use any good paste.

- Glue – use any good glue to stick cardboard and sponge rollers.

- Ink – this is sold by stationery and art stores.

GETTING READY

Printing and painting can be a messy business, so it's a good idea to get everything ready before you start. Cover a table with lots of newspaper and put it over any furniture which could be splashed with paint. If you're making very long prints on rolls of paper, put newspaper on the floor and use it as a work surface. Wear old clothes or something over your clothes. An old shirt makes a good painting smock.

Collect all the things you'll need for one kind of printing and have them ready to use. Rags are useful for wiping paint off your hands and mopping up spilled paint or ink. When you have made a print, hang it up or lay it down flat to dry. Remember to clean up when you've finished printing. Put the tops on bottles and tubes of paint and wash the brushes.

1 MAKING A DABBER

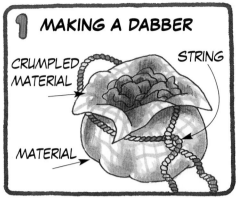

CRUMPLED MATERIAL STRING

MATERIAL

Crumple up a small piece of old material into a ball. Put it in the middle of a small square of material and tie it with string, like this.

2

Dip the dabber in some paint and use it to cover printing blocks evenly with paint.

BRUSHES

When you've finished with a brush, wash it in clean water and dry the bristles with old material, wiping from the handles to the tip. Store brushes standing on the handles.

PRINTING BASE

When you print with vegetables, leaves or with blocks, put a thick wad of newspaper under the printing paper. This will help you to make good, clear prints.

PAPER STRETCHING

When paper gets very wet with water or paint, it sometimes dries in wrinkles. Try this way of stretching paper before you use it for printing. The paper will then dry flat.

1 MAKING A PRINT PAD

Cut out a square of old, thick material. Put it on a flat plate and pour on some paint. Press printing blocks and vegetables on the pad to cover them with paint.

2

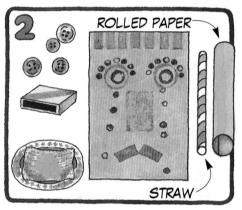

ROLLED PAPER

STRAW

Try using the pad for putting paint on such things as small boxes, straws, buttons, erasers, rolled-up paper and printing with them. Make up a pattern or a picture.

1

BOARD

PAPER

WET SPONGE

Put a sheet of newspaper down on a board or old table top. Rub it gently all over with a clean sponge dipped in clean water.

2

WET PAPER

STRIPS

Wet four strips of gummed paper or masking tape, a little longer than the paper. Press them down on the edges of the paper, sticking it to the board or table. Leave to dry. Pull off the strips.

Finger, thumb and hand prints

The secret of making good fingerprints is to use paint that is not too wet, just sticky. Spread some poster paint on an old tray or plate, or use a print pad (see page 79). Dab your fingers in the paint and press them gently onto a clean piece of paper. If the paint stickiness is just right, it will show up the swirls of tiny lines on your fingertips.

To print bigger shapes, spread paint on a tray or plate. Press down your fists, palms or the sides of your hands and roll backwards and forwards to cover them with paint. When the prints are dry, draw or paint in details to make pictures.

With a magnifying glass you can see that the lines on your fingertips are really grooves and ridges.

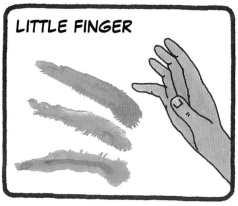

LITTLE FINGER

Curl your little finger and rock it towards the tip as you press it down.

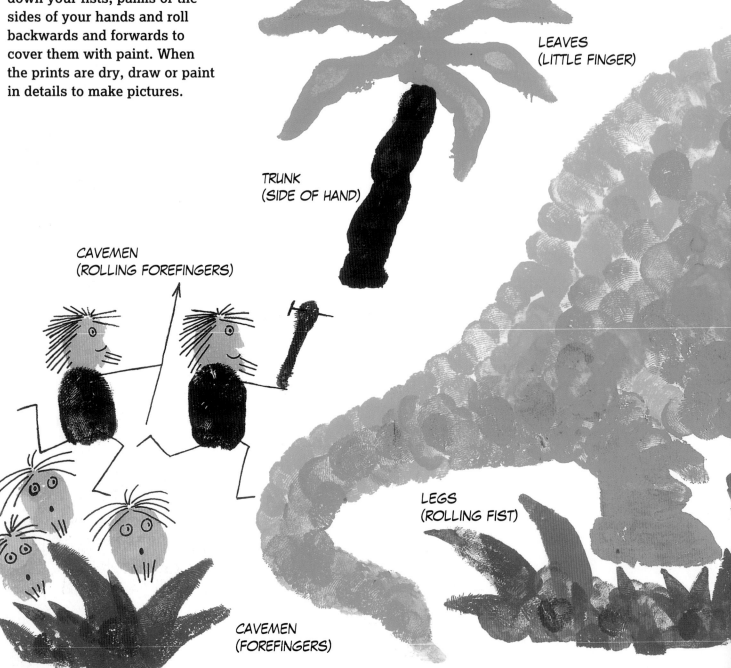

LEAVES
(LITTLE FINGER)

TRUNK
(SIDE OF HAND)

CAVEMEN
(ROLLING FOREFINGERS)

LEGS
(ROLLING FIST)

CAVEMEN
(FOREFINGERS)

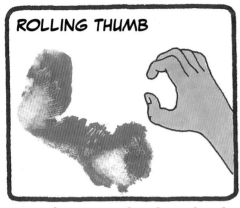

ROLLING THUMB

Press down your thumb, and rock it slightly towards the knuckle.

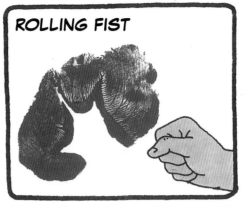

ROLLING FIST

Make a fist and press it down with a rolling movement.

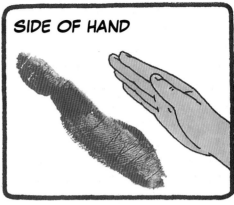

SIDE OF HAND

Press down the side of your hand and rock it from side to side.

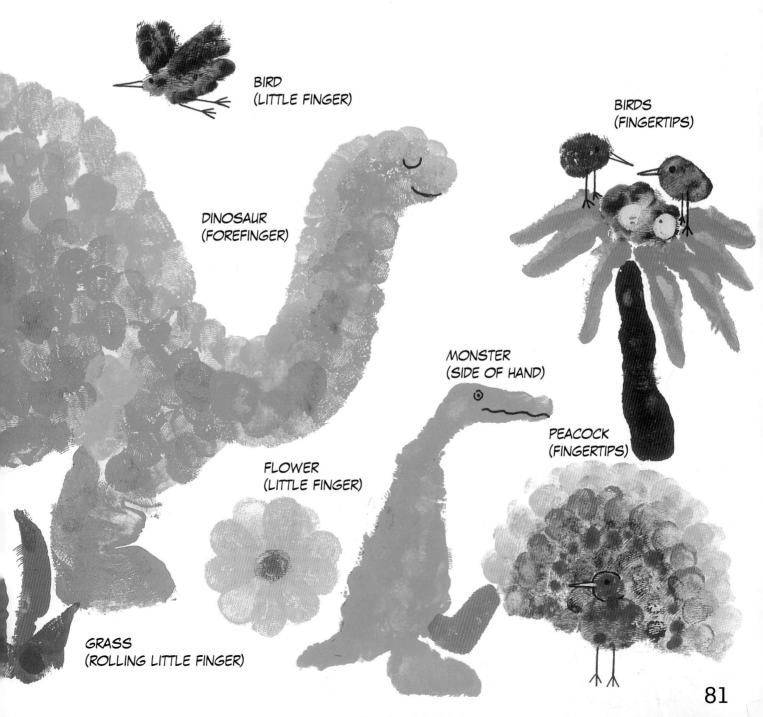

BIRD
(LITTLE FINGER)

BIRDS
(FINGERTIPS)

DINOSAUR
(FOREFINGER)

MONSTER
(SIDE OF HAND)

PEACOCK
(FINGERTIPS)

FLOWER
(LITTLE FINGER)

GRASS
(ROLLING LITTLE FINGER)

Mirror prints

These prints are called mirror prints because the two shapes on either side of the folded paper are exactly the same, like the reflection in a mirror. They are quick and easy to make and every one is different.

YOU WILL NEED

- thick poster paint
- pieces of paper
- pieces of string for string prints
- a paint brush
- an old plate
- newspaper

1 MYSTERY BLOB PRINTS

NEWSPAPER

Fold a piece of paper in half. Open it and drop or flick big blobs of wet poster paint onto one side, near the fold. Use lots of different shades, like this.

MYSTERY BLOB

2

FOLD PAPER OVER

PRESS AND RUB

Fold over the paper so that the clean half touches the paint. Rub the paper hard all over with your hand.

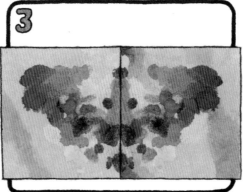

3

Try making lots of blob prints, in different shapes, using lots of shades, like this.

PAINTED PRINT

1 PAINTED PRINTS

Fold a piece of paper in half. Open it and paint a shape or pattern on one side of the paper, near the fold. Use paint that is not too wet.

2

PAINT IN LEAVES

Fold the paper over and rub all over it with the side of your hand. Open the paper and draw or paint in details to make a picture.

82

1 STRING PULL PRINTS

STRING

Pour some thick poster paint onto an old plate. Then, dip a piece of thin string in the paint. Brush the paint over it too, to cover it with paint.

2

DROP ON STRING

Fold a sheet of paper in half. Open it out and drop the painted string onto one side, leaving one end of the string hanging over the edge of the paper.

3

PULL OUT STRING

PRESS

Fold over the paper and hold it down with one hand. Pull out the string hanging over the edge of the paper with the other hand. Now open out the paper.

4

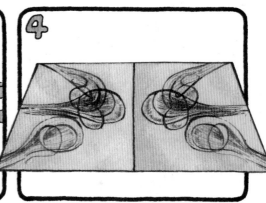

Try dropping lots of pieces of string, each dipped in a different paint, onto the paper. Hold down the folded paper and pull out all the strings at the same time.

1 STRING DROP PRINTS

DROP STRING ON PAPER

Dip a piece of string in some paint, making sure it is well covered. Drop the string on one side of a folded sheet of paper. Fold over the paper and press hard on it.

2

Open up the paper and pick up the string. Let the print dry. Do the same again using a different shade of paint. Do it lots of times until you have an exciting print.

Printing with blocks

Make a printing block and use it as many times as you like. Try printing a border or rows of shapes to make a pattern. When you've printed one shade of paint, wipe the block with a damp cloth and use it again for another shade. Remember, when you print a shape, it will be the other way around from the one you cut out.

YOU WILL NEED

- small blocks of wood
- poster paint
- strong glue
- an old plate or a baking tray
- pieces of paper to print on
- string for string block prints
- thick cardboard for card blocks
- corrugated cardboard for block prints
- newspaper
- scissors

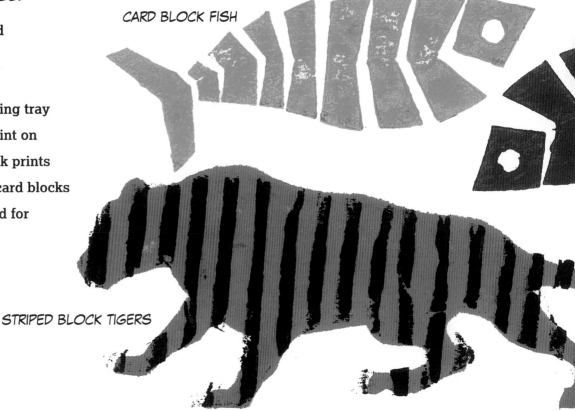

CARD BLOCK FISH

STRIPED BLOCK TIGERS

1 CARD BLOCK PRINTS

Draw a shape, smaller than the block of wood, on a piece of thick cardboard. Cut out the shape in one piece or cut it into lots of different pieces, like this.

2 STICK ON SHAPES

Spread glue over the block of wood. Arrange the shapes on the wood and press them down on the glue. Let the glue dry before starting to print with the block.

3 PRESS

Pour some thick paint onto a tray or plate and spread it out evenly. Dip the block onto the paint, making sure the card shapes are well covered with paint.

STRING BLOCK SNAILS

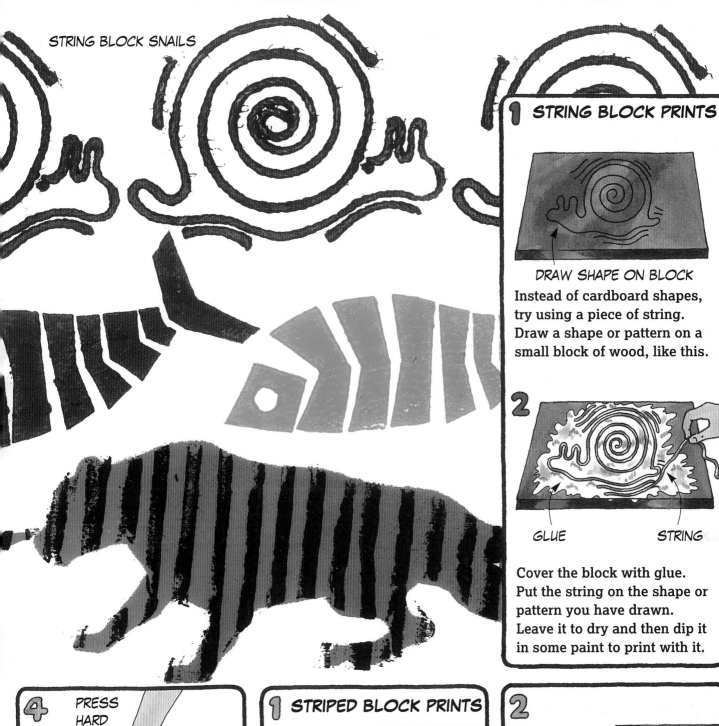

1 STRING BLOCK PRINTS

DRAW SHAPE ON BLOCK

Instead of cardboard shapes, try using a piece of string. Draw a shape or pattern on a small block of wood, like this.

2

GLUE   STRING

Cover the block with glue. Put the string on the shape or pattern you have drawn. Leave it to dry and then dip it in some paint to print with it.

4 PRESS HARD

Put a sheet of paper on top of some layers of newspaper. Press the block onto the paper. Press hard and evenly on the block, like this, to get a good print.

1 STRIPED BLOCK PRINTS

THICK CARDBOARD

Cut a shape out of thick cardboard and glue it to a block of wood. Dip the shape in thick, bright paint and make a print with it on a piece of paper.

2

CORRUGATED CARDBOARD

Cut the same shape out of some corrugated cardboard and glue the flat side to another block of wood. Dip it in a dark paint and press it over the first print.

85

Printing letters

Make these stencil, block and string alphabets to print letters and numbers. Or make up your own letters in any way you like.

YOU WILL NEED

- thick paper for the stencil alphabet
- thick cardboard for the block and string alphabets
- scissors and some string
- a pencil and a ruler
- pieces of paper
- glue
- an old baking tray

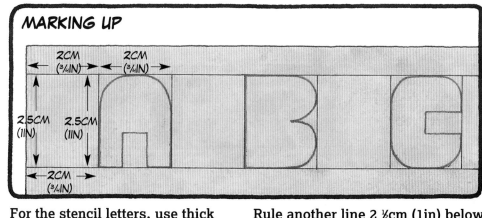

MARKING UP

2CM (¾IN) 2CM (¾IN)

2.5CM (1IN) 2.5CM (1IN)

2CM (¾IN)

For the stencil letters, use thick paper. For the string and block letters, use thick cardboard. First rule a line on the paper or cardboard.

Rule another line 2 ½cm (1in) below it. Put a ruler on the top line, mark off 2cm (¾in) spaces and rule lines as shown. Draw letters of the alphabet in every other space.

STENCIL LETTERS

CUT OUT LETTERS

Draw the letters on a sheet of thick paper and cut out each letter. Be careful not to tear the edges of the letters. Use the stencil to print names and words.

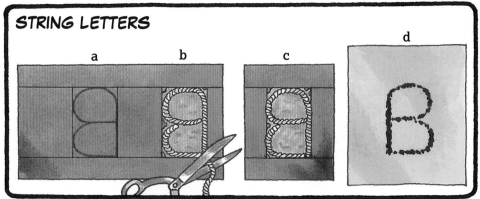

STRING LETTERS

a   b   c   d

Rule lines and draw a letter (a). Spread on glue and press down the string in the shape of a letter. Cut off the extra string (b).

Cut around the letter to make a small square of cardboard, like this (c). Dip the letter in poster paint and print with it (d).

1 BLOCK LETTERS

THICK CARDBOARD

Mark up the alphabet on some thick cardboard and cut out the letters. Put the cut-out letter on another piece of cardboard, draw around it and cut out a second letter.

2

GLUE TOGETHER

Glue the two letters together, like this, to make a very thick cardboard letter. The thickness of it means it will print clearly.

3

Cut out a piece of cardboard a little bigger than the letter. Glue the letter, back to front, onto it. Press the cardboard block in some paint and print with it.

STENCIL AND BLOCK ALPHABET

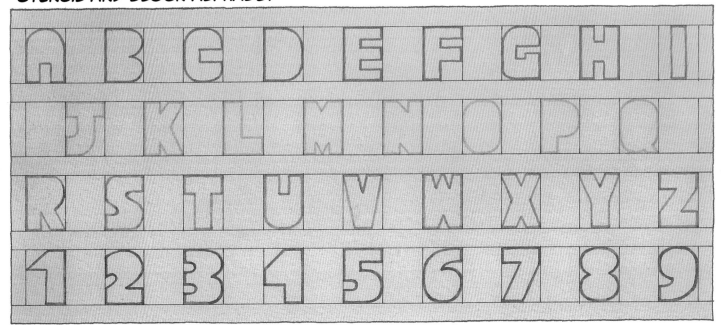

PRINTED STENCIL AND BLOCK ALPHABET

A B C D E F G H I

STRING ALPHABET

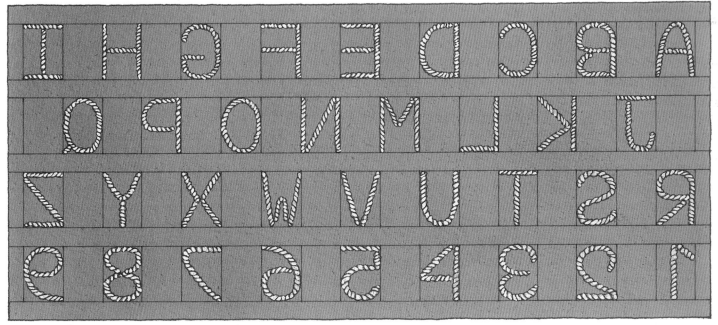

PRINTED STRING ALPHABET

A B C D E F G H I

Scratch pictures

Use lots of bright wax crayons to make these scratch prints. Dark shades will not show up on the black paint or ink. Try scratching animal or monster faces and cut them out to make masks.

YOU WILL NEED

- bright wax crayons
- black poster paint or black drawing ink
- a white candle
- pieces of white paper
- a paint brush

1 PAINT ON WAX PRINTS

Draw thick lines with different wax crayons on a sheet of paper. Press down hard on the crayons so that you make thick bands.

2

BLACK PAINT OR INK

Paint all over the lines with black poster paint or drawing ink. If the wax is difficult to cover, brush on several coats of black paint or ink.

3

When the paint or ink is dry, scratch it off in a shape or pattern with the handle of a paint brush to show the wax underneath.

BLACK AND WHITE PRINTS

Rub white candle wax on a piece of paper. Cover the wax with lots of coats of black poster paint. Let it dry and then scratch off the black paint in patterns.

PAINT ON WAX SNAKE

WAX ON PAINT MONSTER

1 WAX ON PAINT PRINTS

BLACK PAINT OR INK

Paint a shape on a sheet of white paper using black poster paint or black drawing ink.

2

WAX SHAPES

When it's dry, draw patterns all over the black shape with bright wax crayons. Press hard on the crayons to make thick bands.

3

SCRATCH OUT PATTERNS

Use the handle of a paint brush to scratch black patterns and shapes in the bright crayon.

Printing on cloth

You can use fabric dye or waterproof inks to print bright patterns and letters on almost anything. You could try printing on all kinds of materials, clothes and canvas shoes.

Buy water-based fabric dyes which are used with a fixer, and follow the instructions on the bottles very carefully. Dyes are quite expensive so you could just get two or three shades and try mixing them together to make other shades.

Before you start, put down lots of newspaper on the surfaces you are going to work on. If you get dye or ink on any furniture or on the floor, wipe it off immediately. Use a cloth and lots of water or it will stain.

Try the print you're going to do on a scrap piece of material first. Then you can get an idea of how it will look before you do your final print. Make sure any material you use is dry and clean before you begin.

Stretch out the material with your hands before you make a print – a print won't work if the material is crumpled.

Remember to print dark shades on light cloth. Light shades of dye and ink will not show up on dark material.

You can try printing on almost any kind of material but you will get the best results on cotton cloth. Try experimenting with different dyes and materials to find out what works best.

YOU WILL NEED

- water-based fabric dyes and fixer waterproof inks
- pieces of cloth and clothes for printing on
- cookies for cookie prints
- a white candle for wax and dye patterns
- polystyrene (from packaging), cardboard and pins for printing blocks
- a long stick for wall hangings
- string
- needle and thread
- a paint brush and a pencil
- an old baking tray or plate
- lots of newspaper

COOKIE PRINTS

Use a hard cookie with some kind of pattern on it as a printing block. Brush ink or dye on to one side and then make a print on some material or fabric.

WAX AND DYE

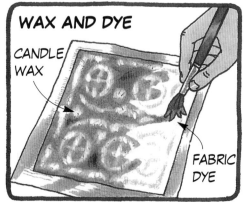
CANDLE WAX
FABRIC DYE

Draw a pattern on a piece of white cloth with a white candle, pressing down very hard. Brush ink or dye over the cloth. It will stay white where the candle lines are.

1 CARD BLOCKS

PIN
CARDBOARD SHAPES

Cut a flower shape out of thick cardboard. Push a pin through the middle and then into the block of thick expanded polystyrene.

2

CARD BLOCK PRINT

Stuff white canvas shoes with newspaper. Brush ink or dye over the cardboard flower and print the shape on the shoes.

T-SHIRTS

FOLDED NEWSPAPER

STENCIL PRINT

Put folded newspaper inside a T-shirt to stop the dye from going through to the other side. Use a stencil to print a pattern or your name in bright ink or dye.

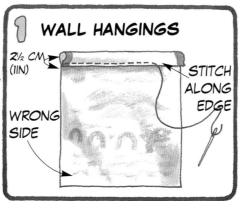

1 WALL HANGINGS

2½ CM (1IN)

WRONG SIDE

STITCH ALONG EDGE

Print a picture in dye or ink on a large white cloth. A piece of old sheet is good for this. Fold over about 2 ½cm (1in) at the top and stitch the edge down, like this.

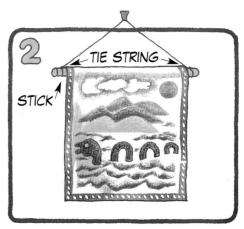

2

TIE STRING

STICK

Push a long stick through the stitched pocket. Tie the ends of a piece of string around each end of the stick and hang the picture up.

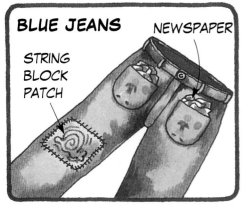

BLUE JEANS

NEWSPAPER

STRING BLOCK PATCH

Print ink or dye patterns on the pockets of light blue jeans or print patches and sew them on. Remember to put newspaper in the pockets before you begin.

SCARVES AND HANDKERCHIEFS

STRING STENCIL LETTERS

SF

SPONGE ROLLER PRINT

Try printing names or initials on handkerchiefs to make presents, or use a sponge roller to print stripes on a scarf.

Poster factory

Several people working together can set up a production line and produce lots of posters quickly. Each person should have a particular job to do. Lay out everything they need. Stack newspapers on the tables. Hang the posters up to dry after each step.

First make the poster borders using a light shade. Then print patterns on top of the border in a darker or brighter shade. Use the stencil, block or string alphabets on pages 86-87 for the lettering on the posters.

YOU WILL NEED

- paper and poster paint
- thick paper for stencils
- a string block (see page 85)
- thick cardboard and some string
- a baking tray and some scissors
- strong glue
- lots of newspaper and cloths to keep everything clean
- potato for potato prints
- wood block prints (you can buy them from art or stationery stores)

CLOTHES PEGS

CLEAN PAPER

NEWSPAPER

BAKING TRAY

CLOTH FOR WIPING HANDS

POSTER BORDERS

WEIGHT

SPONGE ROLLER

You could wrap a sponge cloth around a cardboard tube and make a sponge roller. This is a quick and easy way to paint borders around your posters.

STENCIL BORDERS

Draw a pattern on thick paper. Cut out the pattern. Lay the paper down over the border and dab a second shade through it with a sponge.

ONE-BLOCK POSTERS

Instead of using lots of different prints on a poster, try making a one-block poster. Cut a piece of cardboard the same size as the poster paper.

Mark up the cardboard (see page 86) and glue string letters on to it. Glue a string pattern around the edges. Roll paint over the string letters and print with it.

STRING BLOCK BORDERS

Try making a long poster, like this, and printing patterns around the poster border. You could print it with a string block or a cardboard block.

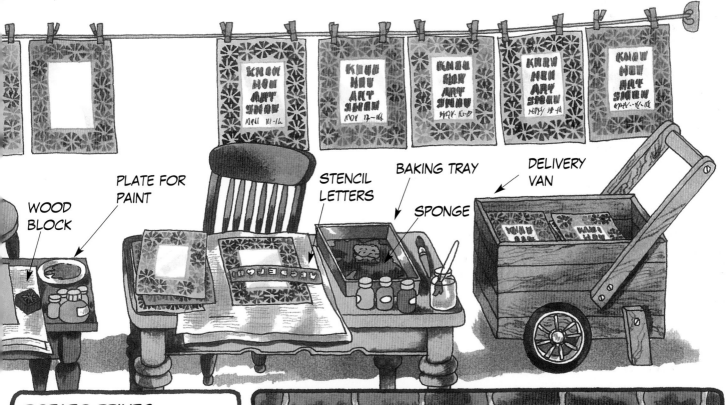

WOOD
BLOCK

PLATE FOR
PAINT

STENCIL
LETTERS

BAKING TRAY

SPONGE

DELIVERY
VAN

POTATO PRINTS

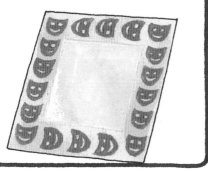

Cut a potato in half and carve out a pattern, such as this face. Dip the potato in paint and print around the border. This poster could advertise a play or a puppet show.

WOOD BLOCK BORDERS

You can buy wood printing blocks with rubber patterns on them from some art or stationery stores. They are great for printing patterns quickly.

When you are making posters remember to use thick paper which will not crumple or wrinkle. Print them with large, simple patterns in bright shades.

Instead of printing borders, try gluing on strips of bright paper. If you hang the posters outside, put them in large see-through plastic bags to keep them dry.

Putting on an exhibition

When you have printed lots of pictures and patterns, try putting on an exhibition. Frame or mount your pictures on bright cardboard first. Here are some ideas on how and where to hang your pictures if you have an outdoor show. For an indoor show, tie string to points in a room and hang the pictures from the string. Send printed invitation cards telling everyone where to come, at what time and whether it will cost them anything. Make posters to advertise the exhibition.

YOU WILL NEED

- printed pictures
- pieces of bright cardboard for frames
- a ruler
- a pencil
- sticky tape
- string
- an old sheet
- scissors
- clothes pegs, paper clips or pins
- posters (see pages 92-93)
- invitation cards

KNOW HOW PRINT SHOW FRIDAY JULY 30TH

1 CARDBOARD MOUNTS

GLUE ON

Dab a little glue on the four corners of the back of the picture. Put the picture down on a sheet of bright cardboard, like this, and rub all over it with your hand.

2

RULE LINES

Put a ruler on the edge of one of the sides of the picture and rule a line in pencil, like this. Do the same with the other three sides of the picture.

3

CUT ALONG LINES

Carefully cut along the four ruled lines with scissors. Put sticky tape loops on the four corners of the back of the cardboard to hang the picture up.

STICKY TAPE LOOPS

STICKY SIDE OUT

Curl a small piece of tape, sticky side out, into a loop and stick the ends together. Put a loop in each corner of a picture to hang it up.

STRING LOOPS

Tape a piece of string to the card on the back of a picture, like this. Hang the picture from the middle of the string.

HOW TO HANG PICTURES

Think how tall the people you are inviting to your exhibition are and hang your pictures so that they are level with the people's eyes. Ask a friend to hold the picture while you stand back to see if it is in the right position. With two rows of pictures, hang one just above eye level and one just below.

1 CARDBOARD WINDOW FRAMES

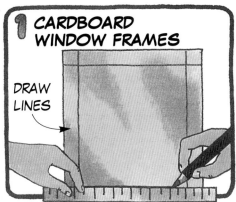

DRAW LINES

To make a window frame, cut a piece of bright cardboard the same size as the picture. Put a ruler on the edges of the cardboard and draw four pencil lines, like this.

2

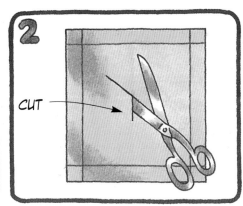

CUT

Cut out the middle of the cardboard by pushing one blade of the scissors through the middle of the card. Cut to one corner and then along the lines you have drawn.

3

PICTURE IN MIDDLE

GLUE ON FRAME

Put a little glue on the four corners of the back of the picture frame. Carefully place the frame on top of the picture and press down with your hands.

95

Party prints

Before you have a party, you can make lots of things for it. Start the day before so that the paint and ink have time to dry.

YOU WILL NEED

- white paper cups, plates and napkins
- pieces of paper
- waterproof inks
- poster paint
- a pencil and scissors
- a sponge and glue

PAPER PLATES

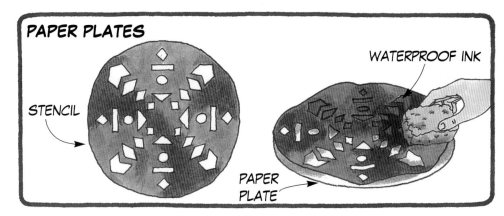

STENCIL

WATERPROOF INK

PAPER PLATE

Put a paper plate down on a piece of paper and draw around it. Cut out the circle and fold it up several times. Cut little pieces out of the folds to make a stencil.

Unfold the stencil and put it down on a paper plate. Use waterproof inks and a sponge to print the stencil in different shades on the plate, like this.

PAPER HATS

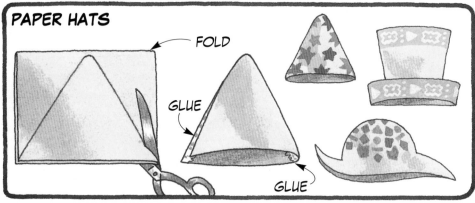

FOLD

GLUE

GLUE

Make a hat by folding a big piece of paper in half. Cut out a hat shape and glue the two pieces together along the top edges. Try cutting out different shapes.

When the glue is dry, decorate both sides of the hats using some of the printing ideas from this section. Use different shades of poster paint and patterns.

PAPER CUPS

STENCIL

Cut a small pattern in a strip of paper to make a stencil. Wrap it around the outside of a paper cup and use waterproof inks and a sponge to print a pattern.

PAPER NAPKINS

Fold napkins into small squares or triangles. Dip corners or edges in waterproof inks. Press the napkins between newspaper. Unfold and hang up to dry.

PAPER MATS

PE

Fold the large sheets of paper in half and cut along the folds. Decorate the edges with a print.

Use string or stencil letters to print the names of each friend coming to the party. Put the mats on the table so everyone knows where to sit.

Detection

Detective headquarters

As a detective, the first thing you must do is set up headquarters (H.Q.). This is where you will keep your reports, your criminal records, your maps of the local area – all the information you will need in order to act quickly when the time is ripe.

A good detective needs a lot of information, and may spend hours walking slowly around the area, getting to know the ground. But the detective will spend even more time at their desk at H.Q., sifting through reports and carefully piecing together facts and clues.

The office may look dusty (police stations never close) but the paperwork must always be in perfect order. There may be twenty cases going at once. The detective may get new information on any of them and must be sure each new report is added to the files. Information is the chief weapon in the battle against crime.

Look around the picture on the right to see what you need to set up headquarters. Below you can see the first thing you need – a warrant card.

THIS IS FUZZVILLE H.Q. IT'S BEEN A SLOW DAY - AND DETECTIVE-INSPECTOR SHAMUS IS GETTING RESTLESS.

SHAMUS

BOX FILE

IT'S JUST TOO QUIET, BILL. ALL THE VILLAINS SEEM TO HAVE GONE UNDERGROUND... OR STRAIGHT. I DON'T KNOW WHAT TO MAKE OF IT! *

NOT EVEN AN ESCAPED MOUSE IN SIGHT

WARRANT CARD

A warrant card is a police officer's identity card.

BACK VIEW

TAPE

PIN

MAKING A WARRANT CARD

Cut out a neat piece of white cardboard (or a cereal box with white paper glued over it). Glue on to it a good head-and-shoulders photograph of yourself. Print your name and the words 'Warrant Card' and sign it in ink.

If possible, cover the card with see-through plastic. Stick a safety pin on the back with sticky tape and pin it behind your collar. Then you can flip back your collar and show it to identify yourself.

BOX FILE

D.I. BLOGGS

A box file is just a handy container for information on the cases you are investigating. Use it to carry things such as, photographs, reports and statements made by witnesses.

DIVISIONAL MAP

BILL

MISSING PERSONS

CRIMINAL RECORDS A/Z

POLICE GAZETTES

STOLEN VEHICLES

SUSPECTS CONVICTIONS

LOST PROPERTY

CRIMINAL RECORDS FILING CABINET

REPORTS

COULD BE WE'VE SORTED 'EM OUT, GUV. THE GEEZER'S IN STIR – ROGER THE DODGER'S GOT BIRD – AND I'LL BET YOU'VE GOT RID OF THE FLAT MAN FOR GOOD, NOW! *

BUT... WHO CAN TELL? A DETECTIVE NEVER KNOWS WHAT CASE MAY BREAK... WHAT TERRIFIED VICTIM MAY WALK THROUGH THE DOOR... WHAT CHANCE BIT OF INFORMATION MAY SEND HIM OFF UPON A NEW (AND POSSIBLY DANGEROUS) ADVENTURE. FOR INSTANCE AT THIS VERY MOMENT...

*DETECTIVE LANGUAGE

Villain – a criminal
Stir – in prison
Bird – a prison sentence
Gone straight – now honest, stopped committing crimes.

POLICE REPORTS

P.C. BEAVER REPORTS SUSPECT CAR NO. XQ0011. SAME TIME EVERY FRIDAY AT BANK OPENING TIME JOHN SMITH (DRIVER) CRO 734/62

All police officers make reports on the information they gather. They clip or 'spike' the reports together, for the person who collects them (known as the collator).

BULLETIN

The collator puts all the reports into a kind of news-sheet. Then each police officer knows what is happening all over the area.

STATEMENT

LOST ALSATION

A cereal box makes an excellent box file. Just be sure to label it with your name along one side, as shown.

NOTEBOOK
WRITE ON EVERY LINE AND LEAVE NO SPACES

Always carry a notebook. Tie on a pencil with some string, like this. Use it to write down useful information.

For example, make notes of suspicious things, such as a car always parked by a bank just at closing time. And try taking statements from people who have seen accidents. Remember – a police officer's notebook may be used in court as evidence. There must be no rubbed out spots. Each page must be numbered. Don't leave any gaps in the writing, even for paragraph breaks.

Reading clues

SHAMUS, YAWNING, STARTS TO FLICK THROUGH THE PAGES OF LAST SUNDAY'S PICTURE NEWS – AND FINDS A STORY WHICH IS SOON TO DOMINATE HIS LIFE...

LOOK AT THAT... A WOMAN I MIGHT HAVE SEEN ANY DAY RIGHT HERE IN FUZZVILLE... AND IT APPEARS THAT SHE MAY BE A RUSSIAN PRINCESS. AH WELL... LIFE REALLY IS STRANGER THAN FICTION..!

TRUE STORY
by SAMANTHA JONES

OVERNIGHT MILLIONAIRESS?
Fuzzville gem expert recognizes local woman's diamond as part of the famous Wozinsky fortune. Can she prove her claim to the rest of the fortune?

THE WOZINSKY DIAMOND

HAVE YOU READ ABOUT THE WOZINSKY HEIRESS? GOSH... I WISH I COULD MEET A PRINCESS!

Esther, Gerald and Olga
June 1923

LITTLE DO THEY EXPECT...

WHAT IS THE STORY OF THE FUZZYVILLE HEIRESS?

A clue is anything that helps you discover new information. It may be very small – a hair or a shiny screw on an old car number plate. A good detective can get lots of information from tiny details. Try this puzzle to test your skill at reading clues.

Shamus has just learned that a Fuzzville woman may be the long-lost heiress to the Wozinsky fortune. Where did the fortune come from? Why didn't she know about it sooner?

The pictures in the magazine show several clues to the Fuzzville woman's story. Study them carefully, noticing things like flags and buildings. (There is one clue you will find in almost every picture.)

Try to work out the story the pictures tell. Turn the page upside-down to find the answer.

ANSWER

Olga was the only child of the Wozinskys, a wealthy Russian family. (Notice the flag and jewels in the first picture.) Their lives were threatened by a revolution in Russia. Olga's mother, disguised as a peasant, asked a visiting English army officer to protect Olga. When she heard his train was wrecked she believed Olga had died.

He adopted Olga, not realizing who she really was – until her diamond brooch was recognized as possibly linking her to the Wozinskys and their fortune.

Examining a witness

A person who has witnessed a crime is often confused and panicky. At first, it may seem impossible to get any facts from him. One of your most important jobs is to calm them down – only then will they be able to remember what they know.

Always start by getting the main facts: the very simple things, like the time and place.

These facts will identify your witness if the case comes to court:

- Day of the week
- Date
- Time
- Place
- Name of the witness
- Address
- Telephone number
- Occupation

These are the most important things you need to know. Going through the list will help calm your witness and help you to keep your cool. Never rely on memory, write down everything your witness says. (Here, Bill is taking notes while Shamus questions Olga.)

Now go on to get a description of the case. Ask your witness how they heard of the case, or why they found themselves at the scene. Ask them what action they took. Again, write it all down.

When you ask for a description of a place or person, your witness may not know where to start. Help them by asking questions, as Shamus does on the right.

Again, start with simple things such as height and weight and get the witness to compare the person with themselves or you. If you can, use examples to jog their memory.

AT THIS MOMENT THE DOOR IS OPENED BY THE VERY WOMAN SHAMUS HAS JUST BEEN READING ABOUT... THE HEIRESS TO THE WOZINSKY FORTUNE.

PRINCESS OLGA!

OH PLEASE... I NEED YOUR HELP. SOMEONE'S AFTER MY INHERITANCE!

AND SHE DESCRIBES HER FEARS...

YOU MEAN THE WOZINSKY FORTUNE? BUT I UNDERSTOOD FROM THE MAGAZINE STORY THAT IT WAS STILL IN A BANK IN SWITZERLAND.

THAT'S TRUE... I CAN'T CLAIM IT UNTIL MY PASSPORT ARRIVES. AND WHAT IF SOMEONE STEALS THE VITAL DOCUMENT MY LAWYER GAVE ME? IT'S THE WOZINSKY'S FAMILY ALBUM, YOU SEE, AND THERE'S A PAGE WITH CHILDISH FINGERMARKS THAT SEEM TO BE INDENTICAL WITH MINE..!

OF COURSE! THE PROOF OF YOUR IDENTITY!

YES... AND I'M SO WORRIED. SINCE THAT STORY IN THE NEWS I'VE BEEN CONSTANTLY PESTERED. A MAN CAME TODAY WHO SAID HE WAS FROM MY LAWYER, BUT I SAW HIM RIFLING MY BUREAU DRAWERS!

I KNOW HE'LL RETURN - I'M SURE OF IT. MAURICE HERE WAS SUSPICIOUS FROM THE START.

MAURICE?

YES, MAURICE HERE - MAURICE WAS **SO** UPSET.

CAN YOU DESCRIBE THE MAN? YOU HAD A GOOD LOOK AT HIM?

HEAVENS, NO... I WAS TOO CONCERNED WITH MAURICE. HE'S STILL OVERWROUGHT, POOR DARLING... HE HAS **SUCH** A SENSITIVE NATURE...

! !

BUT DETECTIVE INSPECTOR SHAMUS HAS FACED THIS KIND OF THING BEFORE.

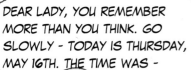

DEAR LADY, YOU REMEMBER MORE THAN YOU THINK. GO SLOWLY - TODAY IS THURSDAY, MAY 16TH. THE TIME WAS -

GRADUALLY, SHAMUS CALMS THE DISTRAUGHT PRINCESS... AND LITTLE BY LITTLE, PRECIOUS FACTS BEGIN TO COME TO LIGHT...

WHEN YOU ANSWERED THE DOOR, DID YOU LOOK UP INTO HIS FACE? OR DOWN?

NOW LET ME THINK. THERE WAS A CUT ON HIS CHIN - YES, I LOOKED UP.

SLOWLY, WITH INFINITE PATIENCE SHAMUS ESTABLISHES THAT THE VISITOR WAS TALL... VERY TALL. A LEAN, SCOWLING MAN WITH THICK, DARK HAIR...

YACKETY YACKETY

Z Z Z Z

AND...

YOU MENTIONED HANGING UP A HAT. COULD YOU DESCRIBE IT? WOULD YOU SAY IT WAS OLD?

NEW?

NO...

BROWN?

YES...

BLACK?

OH NO!

YES -

AND COME TO THINK OF IT, I HAD A QUICK PEEK AT THE LABEL -

THE MAN HAD WORN A BRAND-NEW HAT... SO LARGE IT MIGHT HAVE BEEN BOUGHT TO FIT OVER A THICK GREY WIG...

MOST INTERESTING! BUT LET US LOOK THROUGH THE FILES... PERHAPS YOU CAN IDENTIFY YOUR MAN.

AND TOMORROW, WE'LL GO TO THE BANK WITH THAT VALUABLE ALBUM AND THE DIAMOND.

CERTAINLY, INSPECTOR, CERTAINLY...

LET'S MAKE A START THEN!

AT FIRST GLANCE, NONE OF THE PHOTOGRAPHS ON FILE IN CRIMINAL RECORDS RESEMBLES THE MAN SEEN BY THE PRINCESS... SO SHAMUS BEGINS THE ARDUOUS TASK OF BUILDING AN INDENTIFIT PICTURE TO MATCH OLGA'S DESCRIPTION...

ALL I CAN SAY IS THAT HE HAD A LONG, NARROW FACE, JUTTING JAW, THIN, BEAKY NOSE, TINY EYES AND A VERY SMALL, MEAN MOUTH...

AS THE PICTURE TAKES SHAPE, A DARK SUSPICION GROWS IN SHAMUS' MIND. BUT AS HE PONDERS THE PROBLEM HE MAY BE FACING, OLGA SLIPS AWAY.

COULD IT BE... THE **FLAT MAN?**

I REFUSE TO GIVE UP THE DIAMOND. I CAN HIDE IT... IN A VERY SAFE PLACE..!

How identification kits work

The identification kit used by police works by building up layers of see-through photographs. Each shows just one feature, such as the nose. It is chosen to match what the witness remembers. The layers can be slid up and down to change the face even more, as the witness remembers details.

In a photofit kit there may be hundreds of noses to choose from, so they are sorted into groups. For example, there may be groups of long noses. There are groups of close-together eyes, as well as eyes of different shapes and sizes. There are also lots of different hats and hair styles.

But even one set of features can make several faces, if you squash them close or pull them far apart. Try making the kit shown here, and see what happens when you juggle the bits around. If you have read Olga's description in the story above, you may find a picture of the Flat Man...

HAIR AND FEATURES

104

Is this the man?

CLIP ON THE FACE SHAPE

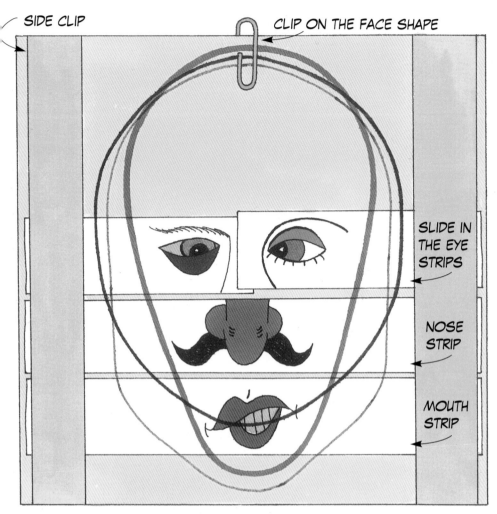

SLIDE IN THE EYE STRIPS

NOSE STRIP

MOUTH STRIP

The red, green and blue lines are all outlines of faces. Trace the face most like the one that Olga describes. Trace some noses, mouths and eyes from the pictures below, and try them on the face. Then turn the page to check your identifit against a genuine picture of the Flat Man.

IDENTIFIT KIT

YOU WILL NEED

- white cardboard
- thin paper or tracing paper
- thick paper for the side clips
- scissors, glue, pencil, paperclips

1. Cut out a big square of cardboard.
2. Cut two strips of thick paper, about 5cm/2in longer than the square. These are the side clips.
3. Fold one end of a strip over the top of the cardboard and glue it down.
4. When the glue is dry, fold over and glue down the other end of the strip, pulling it tight. Attach the other side clip in the same way.
5. To make a face shape, trace the red outline onto a piece of paper about as big as the cardboard. Trace the green and blue outlines separately to make two more shapes.
6. Then trace the 'Hair and features', shown below, onto different strips of paper and fill them in with pencils.
7. To use the kit, clip a face shape over the square and try out different features by sliding them under the side clips. Trace over the whole face on a fresh piece of paper to make a record for your criminal files.

HAT SHAPES

FOLLOWING HIS HUNCH SHAMUS RIFLES QUICKLY THROUGH HIS FILES...

IT MUST BE HIM...

AND SOON FINDS WHAT HE'S BEEN SEARCHING FOR...

PRINCESS! I THINK WE'VE GOT YOUR MAN!

SHE'S GONE, GUV... SLIPPED OUT TEN MINUTES AGO. SAID SOMETHING ABOUT DIN-DINS FOR DARLING MAURICE.

NO! WE'VE GOT TO CONTACT HER... THAT HOUSE MAY BE FULL OF FINGERPRINTS.

WHILE HIS ASSISTANT, BILL, CONTACTS THE PRINCESS, SHAMUS PACES THE OFFICE RESTLESSLY...

IT'S O.K., GUV - SHE HASN'T TOUCHED A THING. SAYS YOU'RE TO COME OVER AND JUST WALK IN. SHE'S LEFT THE DOOR OPEN!

SHE'S WHAT? HOLY MATILDA. HE MAY BE THERE ALREADY!

SHE DOESN'T SEEM TO REALIZE WHO WE MAY BE DEALING WITH.

GREAT SNAKES... THE FLAT MAN!

AND LEAPING INTO HIS FAITHFUL CAR, OLD SUSIE, SHAMUS AND BILL SPEED TO THE HOUSE.

WILL HE BE TOO LATE?

KEEPING RECORDS

As soon as you start working on a case, start keeping records. For example, when you are questioning a witness, you or an assistant should take notes. They may help show if the witness is confused, or lying. When the witness has remembered all he can, he should write a statement, as shown here.

Keep all your notes, papers and evidence together in a box file. Label each item with the case number. It's important to have all the details at your finger-tips.

WRITING A STATEMENT

O. WOZINSKY

Taken by D.S. Wm. WATSON at Fuzzville Police Station between 4:10 and 4:45 on Wednesday 9/9/08

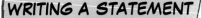

SAMPLE STATEMENT

In a statement, the witness should write down exactly what he knows about the case and sign his name, leaving no spaces where words could be added later. Sign your name, too.

USING CASE NUMBERS

FUZZVILLE DIV.6

CRIME 1/08

SAMPLE LABEL FOR EVIDENCE

Your first case in 2008, will be 1/08. Give each case its own number and use this number on all reports, papers and evidence.

106

Criminal records

What Shamus has just found is the Flat Man's criminal record – the papers that describe him and give details of all his criminal activities. Here is the first page.

A record like this is started for each criminal as soon as he is arrested. You can use this form as a model for your own files – just copy the printed part. Page 110 tells you how to take fingerprints.

Every suspect is given a number when he is first arrested. This is shown on all his records. The number here shows that the Flat Man was the 883rd criminal in Fuzzville (FV) and was first convicted in 1987.

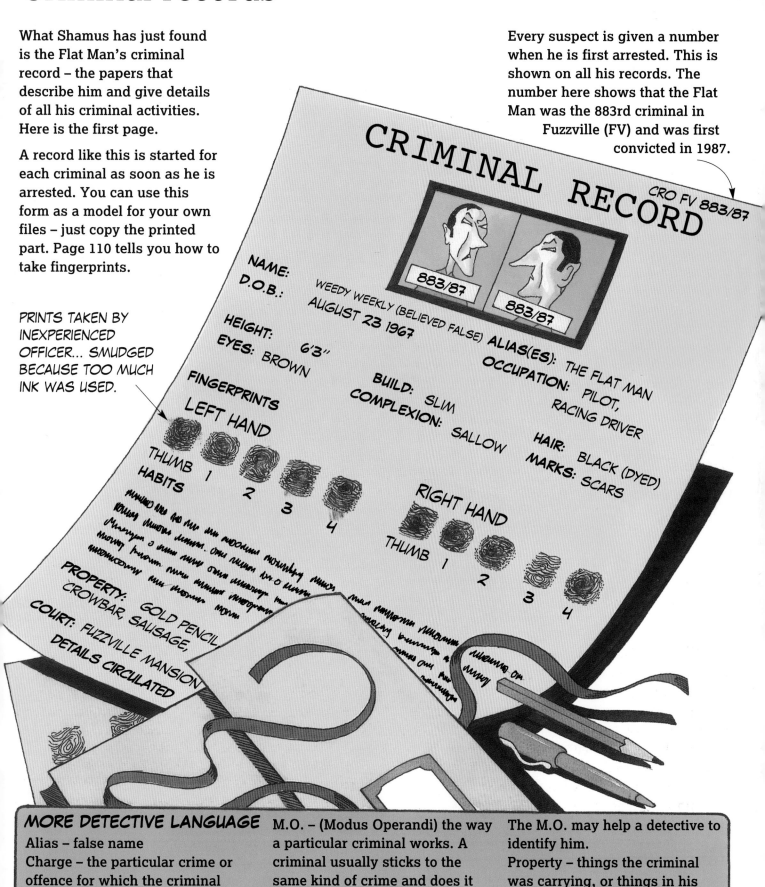

PRINTS TAKEN BY INEXPERIENCED OFFICER... SMUDGED BECAUSE TOO MUCH INK WAS USED.

CRIMINAL RECORD
CRO FV 883/87

883/87   883/87

NAME: WEEDY WEEKLY (BELIEVED FALSE)
D.O.B.: AUGUST 23 1967
HEIGHT: 6'3"
EYES: BROWN
BUILD: SLIM
COMPLEXION: SALLOW
ALIAS(ES): THE FLAT MAN
OCCUPATION: PILOT, RACING DRIVER
HAIR: BLACK (DYED)
MARKS: SCARS

FINGERPRINTS
LEFT HAND
THUMB 1 2 3 4
RIGHT HAND
THUMB 1 2 3 4

HABITS

PROPERTY: GOLD PENCIL, CROWBAR, SAUSAGE,
COURT: FUZZVILLE MANSION
DETAILS CIRCULATED

MORE DETECTIVE LANGUAGE

Alias – false name
Charge – the particular crime or offence for which the criminal was arrested.
D.O.B. – date of birth

M.O. – (Modus Operandi) the way a particular criminal works. A criminal usually sticks to the same kind of crime and does it the same way. If he lies, he usually sticks to the same story.

The M.O. may help a detective to identify him.
Property – things the criminal was carrying, or things in his pockets when arrested.

Searching for fingerprints

The skin of your fingerprints has a pattern of ridges which is special for each person. If you press them on an ink pad and then on paper, you can see the print left by these ridges. The oily sweat on your skin can print the patterns, too. It leaves good prints on polished things like glass or silver – though you need a fingerprint kit to see the details. (The next pages show you how to make one.)

Fingerprints can help you work out who has been at the scene of a crime – but there are tricks to searching for them.

First, when you search a room, be careful not to leave your own prints. Avoid touching anything, even the door, with your finger. Don't think it will be safe if you wear gloves – this can make you careless. Gloved fingers can smudge good prints, and a split in the glove may let the fingerprint through. (This happens to criminals, too.)

Stop and look around when you enter the room. Then search it carefully and thoroughly. Go over it in a circle to make sure you've covered every spot. Make notes of all the places where you see finger-shaped smudges, or where you guess you might find prints. Later you can use your fingerprint kit to develop them (make them show up) and put them in your box files.

Follow Detective Shamus around this picture to see how and where to look for fingerprints in the room. Move along the path shown by the red arrows.

LUCKILY, ALL IS QUIET AT THE HOUSE. THERE ARE NO SIGNS OF AN INTRUDER, AND OLGA HERSELF IS STILL PREPARING HER PET'S MEAL. THE ROOM IN WHICH OLGA SAW HER VISITOR THIS AFTERNOON SEEMS UNDISTURBED. EVEN THE SNACK SHE PREPARED FOR HIM WAITS ON THE TABLE, WHERE SHE LEFT IT WHEN SHE RUSHED TO HEADQUARTERS. AFTER QUESTIONING OLGA CAREFULLY ABOUT WHAT HAPPENED... WHERE THE MAN SAT, AND WALKED, AND WHAT HE DID... SHAMUS HAS A GOOD IDEA OF WHERE TO LOOK FOR FINGERPRINTS. HE BEGINS HIS SEARCH.

OPEN DOOR WITH ELBOWS... THAT'S THE BEST WAY. MUSTN'T TOUCH ANYTHING... LUCKY I DIDN'T HAVE TO TURN THE HANDLE!

NOW CIRCLE THE ROOM... SLOWLY, CAUTIOUSLY... EXAMINING EVERY SURFACE.

THIS GLASS NOW! ANY PRINTS WOULD BE ON THE OUTSIDE! GENTLY EASE THE HAND INSIDE... NOW... SPREAD FINGERS AND LIFT.

AHA! HAM SANDWICHES... THE FLAT MAN'S WEAKNESS! HE CAN'T RESIST A NIBBLE WHEN HE'S ON THE JOB... MUST GET A CAST OF THOSE TEETH MARKS FROM THE LAB!

PRINT-HUNTING PRACTICE

A normal fingerprint is just a delicate grease-mark. Usually it takes a slanting light to show it up. You may get the right light by bending your head, but often you need to pick things up.

Practice examining things without using your fingertips. Use tweezers to lift small things and use a pencil to open and close drawers. Always start at the bottom and work up – then you needn't close each drawer to examine the next one.

To lift a cup or glass, put your fingers inside, as Shamus does. Then open your hand so that it presses against the sides. (Be sure to practice on a plastic cup!)

Be careful to touch things as little as possible. Notice how Shamus uses rulers to close a window. The only point touched is the inside corner of the frame – a place where you would never find a print. You can use this trick to open a window too. Always push into the corner – not straight up or down – and push both corners.

With practice you will find lots of ways to move things without touching them. Pencils and tweezers are useful, but you may want to invent your own tools too – like loops of wire, or hooks for lifting things.

Work with a friend to exchange ideas and have contests. Go around a room together and see who is the first to find a fingerprint in each part of it.

Keep in mind the likely spots, like T.V. buttons and light switches. Smooth, polished things show the best prints.

Fingerprint kit

Here is what you need for a fingerprint kit.

You can make a dark powder from pencil lead. First, sharpen the pencil. Then, holding the pencil over some paper, use the pencil sharpener to carefully grind the tip. Do this by gently pressing the tip against the blade of the sharpener. Pour the powder into a container – you will only need a little.

For practice, try developing your own prints. First rub your fingertips in your hair to make them oily. Then press them firmly on white paper. Use pencil powder to develop them.

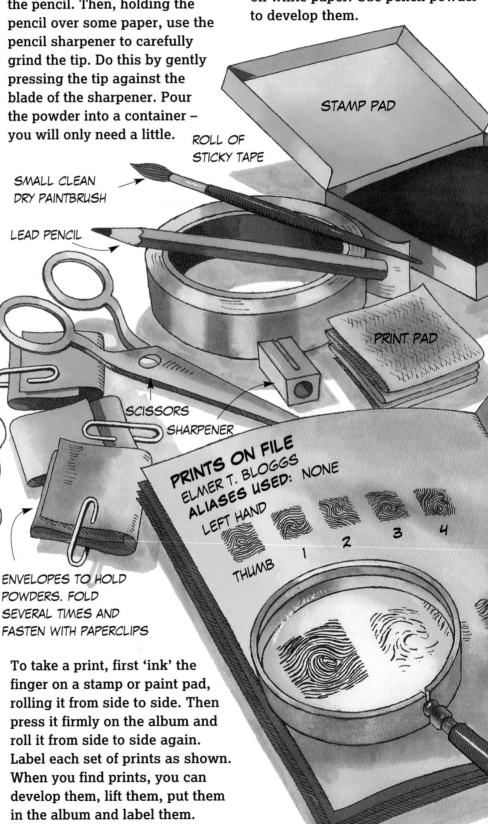

To take a print, first 'ink' the finger on a stamp or paint pad, rolling it from side to side. Then press it firmly on the album and roll it from side to side again. Label each set of prints as shown. When you find prints, you can develop them, lift them, put them in the album and label them.

Make an album from a scrapbook. Start by taking prints from all your family – then search for prints to develop and compare. The next pages show you how to examine the prints.

If you don't have a stamp pad, make a paint pad. Use a piece of cloth, folded several times. Pour on poster paint until the pad is soaked. Press the finger lightly on the pad and roll it from side to side.

...T PRINTS
...ND TIME: 10:00AM APRIL 26TH 2008
...CE:- TOP AND SIDES OF T.V. SET
N FRONT LIVING ROOM IN HOME OF
DOCTOR WEIGHT,
4B HOLMES DRIVE,
CAMBRIDGE.

WHERE DISCOVERED ON T.V.

MAGNIFYING GLASS

FINGERPRINT ALBUM

1 DEVELOPING PRINTS

LEAD POWDER HERE

TALCUM HERE

Use talcum powder on dark things and pencil lead on light things. Dip the brush in and gently shake off any extra powder.

2

Brush the powder very lightly from side to side over the spot where you expect to find a print. Be sure to cover a fairly big area.

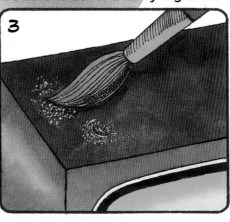
3

Clean the brush by blowing on it or wiping with a tissue. Then carefully brush the loose powder away from the print.

1 LIFTING PRINTS

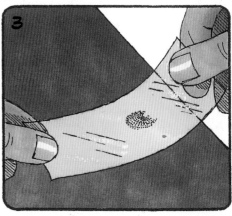

PRESS FIRMLY

Unroll a length of tape and press it carefully on to the developed print. Then cut the tape.

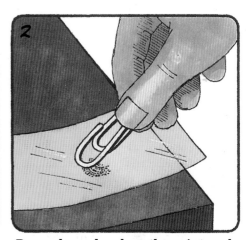
2

Press down hard on the print and rub it well with your fingernail or a paper clip. This brings the pattern of powder on to the tape.

3

If you peel off the tape carefully, the print will come up, too. You will see it again when you stick the tape down again. Always stick talcum prints on dark paper.

Examining fingerprints

A fingerprint is one of the most deadly clues a criminal can leave.

First of all, each fingerprint is unique. The tiny ridges of skin on a fingerprint make a pattern that is different from any other in the world. Even identical twins have different fingerprints.

Second, your fingerprints never change. No matter how old you are, your prints will always reveal your true identity.

Some criminals have tried to burn and cut away their prints, but when the skin grew back, the patterns came to light again...

Try examining some fingerprints yourself – the main shapes are shown below.

On the right, you can see how Detective Shamus examines the prints left by the Flat Man. Could you identify the fingerprints too? Try the puzzle on page 113.

MATCHING FINGERPRINTS

Take prints of your family and sort them into groups like these – arches, loops, whorls and mixed. (Police files use these groups.) Then find and develop a print from somewhere in your house. See if you can work out whose it is.

Get paper and pencil for taking notes, a metal pointer or a sharp pencil for counting ridges and, if you can, a magnifying glass that magnifies two times.

Now work on the subject print:

1. Decide which group the print belongs in (arch, whorl, loop or mixed).

2. Check for identifying marks like cuts and scars.

3. Match the deltas, or any other small shapes you notice.

4. Count the lines (or ridges) between these shapes, to see if the number is the same.

When counting, always start at the middle shape and work outwards until you reach a new shape or odd-looking ridge. Make a quick sketch of it. Then go back to the middle and work outwards in a new direction. Always follow a pattern (clockwise or anti-clockwise) and keep notes as you work. The notes might look like this:

1. Whorl

2. Small cut lower left

3. 34 lines between right-hand edge of whorl and the next shape. (Draw the shape.)

ARCH

This pattern is called an arch, because the shape in the middle is like an arch. The ridges around it are arch-shaped too.

WHORL

A pattern with a line that curls up in the middle is called a whorl. It may be circular or long. It always has two deltas, one each side.

LOOP

The middle line in a loop looks like a hairpin. When you find a loop, you will always find a shape called a delta. The ridges repeat until they get to the delta.

MIXED

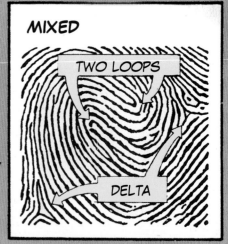

There are many kinds of mixtures. One of the commonest is a double-loop. The line right in the middle bends back upon itself.

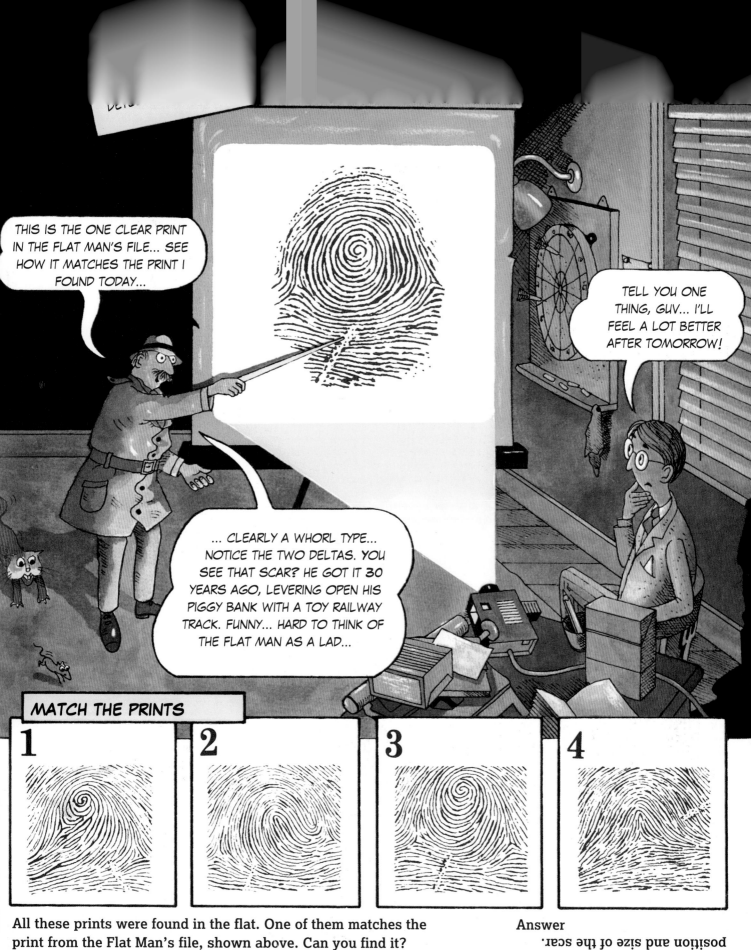

MATCH THE PRINTS

All these prints were found in the flat. One of them matches the print from the Flat Man's file, shown above. Can you find it? There should be four ways in which the two prints match, and no big differences. (Turn the page upside-down to see the answer.)

Answer

ɹɐɔs ǝɥʇ ɟo ǝzıs puɐ uoıʇısod
ǝɥʇ puɐ 'ɐʇlǝp ɥɔɐǝ ɟo uoıʇısod
ǝɥʇ 'lɹoɥʍ ǝɥʇ ǝɔıʇoN ·sǝɥɔʇɐɯ ٤ ·oN

Police escort

Police are often asked to protect valuable things or Very Important People (sometimes called V.I.P.s) as they are taken from place to place. This is called an 'escort'. The police stay close to the V.I.P., ready to shield him or her from attack and clear of danger.

It may take years of practice to get a feel for all the places where danger might be, and the kinds of ordinary-looking event which may really be the start of a clever attack. However, it will help if you remember these main points:

1. Two people make a good escort team – one to walk just ahead of the V.I.P., one behind.

2. Be especially cautious at corners and points where you can't see the route ahead.

3. Steer clear of possible hiding places like doorways.

4. Stay alert at all times.

ESCORT PRACTICE

For escort practice, you need at least three people. One is the detective, one is the crimimal, and one is the V.I.P.

Pin some paper to the V.I.P.'s shoulder to make a target. The criminal needs a felt-tip pen to mark it with. Plan a route with start and finish points. Give the criminal five minutes to hide. Then, as the escort walks past, the criminal tries to mark the V.I.P.'s paper badge. The detective can stop him by shouting 'Criminal Alert!' before he strikes. He must hide again after each try, whether he strikes or is caught. (This can be a game if you take turns. The detective whose V.I.P. gets the least shoulder marks from Start to Finish is the winner.)

AND SO... THE FOLLOWING MORNING THE PRINCESS IS ESCORTED TO THE FUZZVILLE BANK TO DEPOSIT HER VALUABLES. AFTER LOCKING OLD SUSIE, SHAMUS GLANCES QUICKLY AROUND AND STARTS TOWARDS THE BANK. ALL SEEMS NORMAL.

OLD SUSIE

VALUABLES

AS SHAMUS PUSHES THROUGH THE BANK'S REVOLVING DOORS, HE TURNS TO HIS COMPANIONS WITH A SMILE OF RELIEF...

WHICH QUICKLY CHANGES TO A GRIMACE OF ALARM...

NICE DOGGIE!

THE VILLAINS STRIKE WITH DEADLY SPEED...

JAM THE REVOLVING DOOR...

AND MAKE THEIR GETAWAY...

Call-up

As a detective, there may be times when you need help fast. This is when you use a radio call-up.

Every police officer has a two-way radio which links him to radio control (the operator shown in the middle, below). With the flick of a switch, he can use his radio to contact control. If he says 'Emergency!' control stops all other calls to take his message.

Control can broadcast calls for help to every police radio in the area.

Your radio calls should be short and clear. Begin with the code for control (FV for Fuzzville) and give your number or name and rank. For instance, 'FV from 663, a message, 663 over'. (The word 'over' means you have finished speaking.) In a crisis, start by saying 'emergency'.

When spelling names or giving car numbers, it may be hard to say the letters clearly. Use the international call-up alphabet shown on the right. In this, an easy-to-hear word stands for each letter.

CALL-UP ALPHABET

A – Alpha	N – November
B – Bravo	O – Oscar
C – Charlie	P – Papa
D – Delta	Q – Quebec
E – Echo	R – Rome
F – Foxtrot	S – Sierra
G – Golf	T – Tango
H – Hotel	U – Uncle
I – India	V – Victor
J – Julia	W – Whiskey
K – Kilo	X – Xray
L – Lima	Y – Yankee
M – Mike	Z – Zebra

Using this alphabet, the car number 'JFB3H' is Juliet Foxtrot Bravo 3 Hotel.

AS SOON AS SHAMUS IS FREED, HE BEGINS A RADIO CALL-UP... AND WITHIN MINUTES, THE NET IS CLOSING...

CALLING ALL CARS FROM FZ...

SET UP ROAD-BLOCKS...

ALERT PATROL CARS...

ALERT CYCLE COPS...

BRING IN POLICE DOGS...

THE DIAMOND! IT'S NOT HERE!

THEN IT'S BACK TO THE HOUSE, BABY. BUT FIRST...

CAN EVEN THE SPEEDING MASEROONI J8 ESCAPE THE TRAP THAT IS BEING SET..?

Know your scene

You must know your local area thoroughly to set up a roadblock. You must know the times and places where traffic might be heavy and where the criminals might slip through the net. You must know every one-way road and short cut, to plan where your team should be waiting.

Once a call-up starts, you should be able to seal off the area in a matter of minutes.

Unfortunately, experienced criminals expect this – and plan for it. A criminal usually tries to dump his getaway car, and switch to a different kind of car, before he hits the roadblock.

But the abandoned car may hold a vital clue, such as a set of fingerprints – or it may help pinpoint the criminal's exact whereabouts. The sooner you find the car, the more useful it will be to your investigation.

When you are searching for a getaway car, try to put yourself into the criminal's place. What do you think his final destination is – a river, an airport, a main road to somewhere else? What dangers must he avoid, such as crowds and traffic? Where might he find a spot to switch his car without being seen?

A good map of the area is all-important. Below you can see how to mark it.

PREPARING A MAP

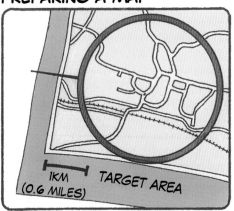

First get a map of your area. Try the local library, a bus station or the Internet. Mark in red the main target for criminal attack – the bank or the jewel store.

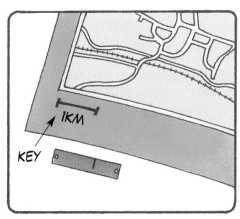

Use the 'key' or 'legend' in the corner of the map to measure a strip of cardboard that stands for 2km (1.2 miles). Make a small hole at each end of the strip.

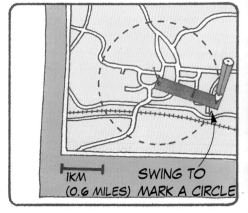

Stick a pin through one hole into the 'target' area. Stick a pencil through the other hole. Swing it to make a circle. This shows where your roadblock should be set up.

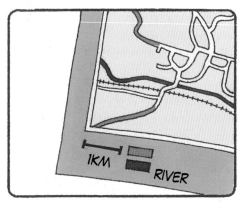

Use bright pencils to mark points the criminals might head for, such as rivers and roads that lead to airports. Then glue the map to a piece of cardboard.

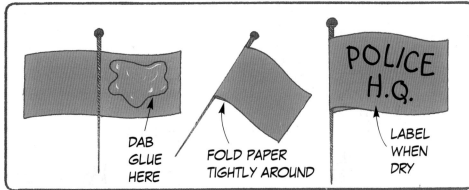

Make flags, like these ones above, to mark all the spots you may need to know in an emergency – such as your local hospital, police and fire stations.

Then search the area for suitable spots to dump a getaway car, such as warehouses. Mark taxi-ranks or train stations; the criminal may need them if his car-swap fails.

Find the getaway car

Now that the alarm has been given, the Fuzzville police are looking for the Maserooni J8. They have a description of the car, the criminals and the car number plate. In any case, a Maserooni is hard to miss. But this, of course, is part of the Flat Man's plan.

Like all experienced criminals, the Flat Man knows he must get rid of his getaway car very fast. Knowing the car will have been spotted heading east for the main road, he is now making his way back towards the bank.

Below you can see the area inside the roadblock. Somewhere in the area the Flat Man must dump the Maserooni and begin the next stage of his getaway. Can you work out where and how he will do it? (Page 127 shows the answer.)

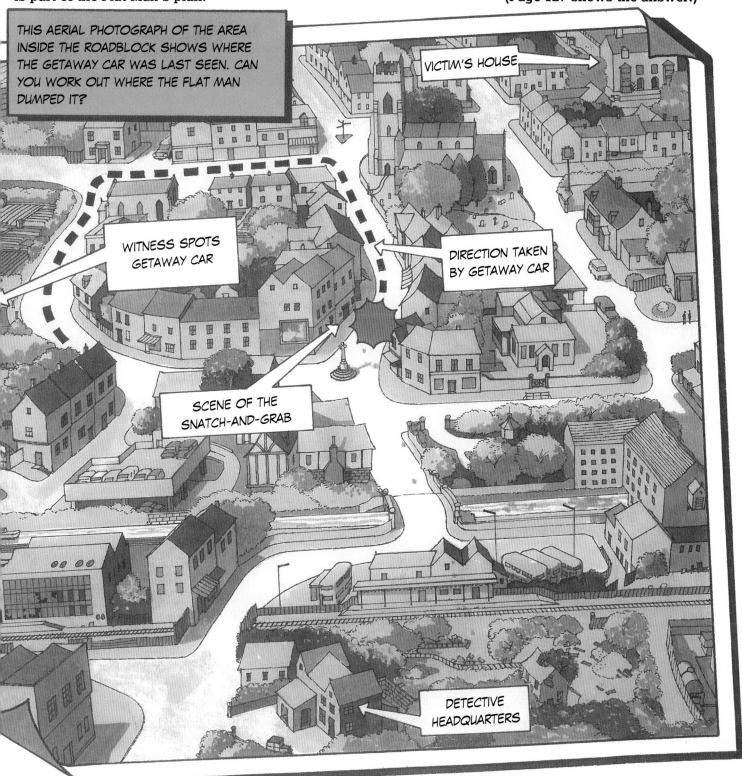

THIS AERIAL PHOTOGRAPH OF THE AREA INSIDE THE ROADBLOCK SHOWS WHERE THE GETAWAY CAR WAS LAST SEEN. CAN YOU WORK OUT WHERE THE FLAT MAN DUMPED IT?

VICTIM'S HOUSE

WITNESS SPOTS GETAWAY CAR

DIRECTION TAKEN BY GETAWAY CAR

SCENE OF THE SNATCH-AND-GRAB

DETECTIVE HEADQUARTERS

Using clues

Even the most experienced criminal often gives himself away by tiny clues left at the scene of the crime. Some clues may give you a good idea of who (or where) the criminal is. (This is called a 'lead'.) Clues may also be used as evidence (to help prove your case in a law court).

Anything the criminal left or marked or disturbed may turn out to be an important clue – if you know how to use it. Keep each clue in a plastic bag and label it. (The police make plaster casts of things like teethmarks and footprints.) Follow Bill around the laboratory on the right to see some of the ways science can help.

POLICE PHOTOGRAPH TAKEN AT THE SCENE OF THE CRIME

FIND THE CLUES

The villains who snatched Olga's valuables have left at least four clues at the crime scene. Can you find them?

READING FOOTPRINTS

To get clues from footprints, you need to study them. Try with several pairs of shoes, like those shown below. Try to work with friends who are bigger, smaller or a different weight, so you can compare prints. Work on damp sand or fine, damp earth and rake or smooth it before you start. Be very careful not to pack it down.

First walk on it normally, in different pairs of shoes. Measure each sole and compare it to its print. Then try running and limping in the same shoes and see where the shoe presses down. Try a standing jump to see where your toes dig in. Notice what happens if you are carrying a heavy load.

ANSWERS

1. **Wig** (one of the criminal's hairs may have stuck to it)
2. **Cap** (same reason – the criminal may have worn it on his real hair)
3. **Footprint** (see below on what footprints can show)
4. **Piece of wood** (see what the wood shows on the right)

Notice that a shoe may print the maker's name or trademark. The maker of the shoes will have a list of stockists (places that sell their shoes). You could visit the stockist and ask questions. If you know the brand and size, someone may remember the people who bought the shoes. This could help narrow down your list of suspects.

COMPARE THESE SHOES AND SHOE-PRINTS

HIGH HEEL

SHOE WITH HEEL

SMOOTH-SOLED SANDAL

RUNNING SHOE

WALKING BOOT

GUM BOOT

OLD SHOE WITH WORN HEEL AND SOLE

SMALL NEW SHOE

LARGE NEW SHOE

SMALL OLD SHOE

LARGE OLD SHOE

SMALL NEW SHOE

LARGE NEW SHOE

NOTICE HOW THE SHAPE CHANGES AS THE SHOE GETS OLD.

SHAMUS DIRECTS OPERATIONS AT THE SCENE OF THE SNATCH, HE KEEPS IN TOUCH WITH RADIO CONTROL. AT LAST...

THEY GOT AWAY, GUV... WE FOUND THE CAR. THEIR BOILER SUITS WERE INSIDE.

I'LL TAKE A LOOK AT THE GETAWAY CAR... YOU TAKE THIS STUFF TO THE LAB, BILL.

IN FUZZVILLE'S FORENSIC SCIENCE LABORATORY...

RUSH JOB I'M AFRAID!

AGAIN? YOUR GOVERNOR SENT SOME PACKETS FROM THE HOUSE LAST NIGHT.

RIGHT, PRIORITY CRIME. STOP EVERYTHING AND START ON THIS STUFF!

DO YOU HAVE ANYTHING FROM LAST NIGHT?

OH YES... EVERYONE HAS BEEN BUSY.

WANT A SANDWICH?

WE GOT A GOOD CAST OF THE BITES.

PLASTER CAST

THE TEETHMARKS ARE DEFINITELY THE FLAT MAN'S. HMMM... CLEVER OF SHAMUS TO SPOT HIS M.O.!*

*M.O. - MODUS OPERANDI (THE FLAT MAN IS A NERVOUS NIBBLER.)

BILL WATCHES EAGERLY AS THE WORK BEGINS...

THE CRIMINAL'S CAP IS CAREFULLY UNSTITCHED (A HAIR COULD BE INSIDE).

AS THE WIG IS EXAMINED FOR ANY LOOSE HAIRS THAT MAY BELONG TO THE CRIMINAL...

AS EACH HAIR IS MOUNTED BETWEEN GLASS SLIDES, TO GO UNDER A MICROSCOPE...

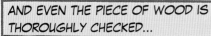

AND EVEN THE PIECE OF WOOD IS THOROUGHLY CHECKED...

LOOK AT THIS SMEAR OF PAINT BILL. I'LL BET IT'S MEANT TO HIDE SOMETHING!

UNDER AN ULTRA-VIOLET LAMP, THE NAME OF A BUILDER'S YARD SHOWS BENEATH THE PAINT...

MUST BE A REASON WHY IT WAS PAINTED OUT. ANOTHER LEAD...?

AT LAST, BILL RETURNS TO H.Q. WITH THE REPORTS. BUT HIS DAY ISN'T OVER YET...

COME TO OLGA'S HOUSE THERE'S BEEN A BREAK-IN

SHAMUS

The scene of the crime

Try to keep calm when you face the confusion left at the scene of a crime. A lot may depend on what you notice and what you do. Keep these rules in mind.

1 LOOK FIRST - DON'T TOUCH

Don't touch anything until the scene has been examined and dusted for fingerprints.

2 FOLLOW A METHOD

Make your examination step-by-step. Look for fingerprints first. Use your kit to pick up any prints you find. Slowly circle the room again. Look for anything the criminal might have touched or left behind.

3 USE YOUR NOTEBOOK

Write down everything interesting you see. Don't leave out any detail that might be useful. Remember: what you notice and write down may be used as evidence.

4 CLUES AND EVIDENCE

The next page shows tips on gathering evidence.

5 TAKE FULL STATEMENTS

Ask victims and witnesses to tell you everything they can (see page 102), and write it down. Take the full name and address of any person mentioned.

Remember, it may be a long time until your case goes to court. Your notebook must give a complete picture of what happened today.

6 SEARCH THOROUGHLY

Now it doesn't matter if you disturb things. Look everywhere – even in drainpipes – for anything the criminal might have left. (Even the stub of a train ticket might give you an important lead.)

7 WORK OUT A STORY

From the start, try to work out what happened, to get an idea of what to look for.

AT OLGA'S HOUSE, BILL RUSHES PAST A POLICE PHOTOGRAPHER AND A FINGERPRINT MAN, AND FINDS SHAMUS IN THE BEDROOM...

WHAT A MESS... WHAT HAPPENED?

MUST BE THE SAME BUNCH WHO DID THE SNATCH. THEY WERE AFTER THE DIAMOND... THE PRINCESS LEFT IT HERE.

I COULDN'T BEAR TO PART WITH IT. I HID IT IN A VERY SAFE PLACE.

Collecting evidence

Which ball broke the window? The position of the evidence may give you a clue. (Check your answer on page 127.)

BALL NO. 1
2M (6.5FT) FROM DOOR 1.8M (6FT) FROM NORTH WALL.

BALL NO.2
2.7M (9FT) FROM EAST WALL 3.5M (11.5FT) S.W. OF TREE

BROKEN GLASS SCATTERED AS FAR AS 1M (3FT) INSIDE OF DOOR.

Put each piece of evidence in a plastic bag. Don't touch it – use tweezers. Or push it onto some cardboard, then into the bag.

Before you remove the evidence, take a photograph or make a sketch to show where you found it. The exact position may be vital. Give at least two measurements, as shown, to pinpoint a position. Measure from things, like walls or trees, that stay in the same spot.

Label the bag to show the case-number and your name. Later you can examine the evidence more thoroughly.

SAFE?

I NEVER DREAMED THEY'D LOOK UNDER THE MATTRESS!

WELL, THE STORY'S CLEAR ENOUGH! WHILE THE PRINCESS WAS HELPING US AT H.Q. THEY ABANDONED THE GETAWAY CAR, BROKE INTO THE HOUSE, AND GOT THE DIAMOND. THE SOIL UNDER THE WINDOW IS COVERED WITH FOOTPRINTS. AND WE FOUND A TRACE OF PAINT ON THE CARPET. IF MY HUNCH IS RIGHT IT'LL TIE IN WITH THIS MORNING'S JOB!

BUT WE KNOW IT'S THE FLAT MAN... DON'T WE?

I'M NOT SO SURE. JUST TAKE A LOOK AT THIS!

BUT THIS IS AMATEUR STUFF! THIS LOT OF DRAWERS WERE OPENED TOP TO BOTTOM... THE FLAT MAN DOESN'T OPERATE LIKE THAT.

RIGHT! AND THE PRINCESS CLAIMS THAT CLOTHES ARE MISSING. NOTICE THE OPENED PERFUME BOTTLES... LONG BLONDE HAIR IN THE COMB... AND UNDER THE LEFT-HAND SET OF DRAWERS WE FOUND...

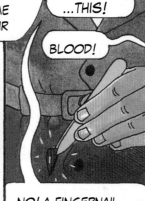

...THIS!

BLOOD!

NO! A FINGERNAIL... WITH BLOOD-RED NAIL POLISH!

IF IT'S THE FLAT MAN, HE MUST HAVE AN ACCOMPLICE! WE KNOW IT'S AN AMATEUR, AND PROBABLY A WOMAN.

BUT WHO? AND WHY?

MEANWHILE, IN A SECRET HIDEAWAY, THE VILLAIN KNOWN AS 'THE FLAT MAN' IS HARD AT WORK... PREPARING A CLEVER TRICK. AS HE BENDS OVER HIS TASK, A FEMALE VOICE SINGS OUT...

HAVE YOU UNSTITCHED THE PAGE?

WOZINSKY FAMILY ALBUM

YEAH... ALMOST!

HAND IT OVER. I'LL KEEP IT IN MY HANDBAG... JUST IN CASE.

HOW ABOUT THE FORGERY?

I'M JUST DABBING ON SOME FAKE FINGERPRINTS...!

WELL?

I DON'T LIKE IT, BABE... BEFORE THIS, I ALWAYS WORKED ALONE.

AH, BUT YOU NEED ME, DON'T YOU? COULD YOU IMPERSONATE* THE PRINCESS?

*IMPERSONATE - TRY TO LOOK AND ACT LIKE A CERTAIN PERSON.

NOW THEN, STITCH THIS PHONEY PAGE IN THE ALBUM, AND WE'LL BE READY!

IS THE HELICOPTER READY?

YEAH, THE 'COPTER'S WAITING!

WE'VE GOT IT ALL! FORGED PASSPORT... THE ALBUM WITH THE DOCTORED PAGE... THE DIAMOND AND TOMORROW...

...THE WOZINSKY FORTUNE!

WHO IS THIS WOMAN?

122

Interpol

Many dangerous criminals roam from country to country in their search for riches – and their flight from detection. They try to escape to places where they are unknown.

They can only be stopped if the police of different countries band together, exchanging help and information. This is the purpose of the International Criminal Police Organization – known as Interpol.

Nearly all the countries in the world belong to Interpol. Each country is ready to share its information with the others and take up the hunt when a criminal is thought to have crossed its borders.

Interpol has a huge database of information. It stores millions of names, fingerprints and DNA profiles. It also keeps details of stolen property, such as passports and works of art. This vast communication system allows important criminal information to be shared quickly and efficiently.

Interpol has its headquarters in Lyon in France. Once a year it holds a meeting, where representatives are sent from each country to discuss crime problems shared by everyone.

MEANWHILE, AT FUZZVILLE DETECTIVE HEADQUARTERS...

WHOEVER THE VILLAINS ARE THEY'LL SOON BE HEADING FOR SWITZERLAND TO CLAIM THE FORTUNE. WE'VE GOT TO STOP THEM.

INTERPOL!

RIGHT AGAIN, OLD BILL. GET ME INTERPOL HEADQUARTERS.

WITHIN MINUTES A CALL GOES OUT FROM LONDON TO FRANCE...

...THEN FROM FRANCE TO EVERY COUNTRY ON THE SWISS BORDER. SOON THE POLICE OF EACH COUNTRY HAVE A DESCRIPTION OF THE CRIMINALS.

WHILE THE FAMOUS OLD SWISS BANK THAT GUARDS THE WOZINSKY FORTUNE IS IMMEDIATELY PUT ON THE ALERT.

SHAMUS HIMSELF WARNS THE MANAGER OF THE SWISS BANK...

BE ON YOUR GUARD FOR IMPOSTORS!

BUT, MONSIEUR SHAMUS, I HAVE JUST HAD A CALL FROM PRINCESS OLGA. SHE IS ARRIVING TOMORROW MORNING AT 11:00.

THIS IS SERIOUS... IT MUST BE THE FLAT MAN'S ACCOMPLICE. SHE'LL BE STAKING HER CLAIM IN LESS THAN 15 HOURS.

OH! IT'S TOO DREADFUL! AND ONLY TODAY MY PASSPORT ARRIVED!

BUT THAT'S A PIECE OF LUCK. YOU'RE COMING WITH US... TO SWITZERLAND.

THAT NIGHT...

I TELL YOU, BILL... THIS TIME I'M GOING TO TRAP THEM.

YOU MEAN... A STAKEOUT?

Stakeout

A stakeout is a police-trap. It is set up when detectives know a certain target will be attacked. They plan things so that the villains can get into the trap without spotting the detectives – but can't get out.

Detectives near the target may be disguised as shop assistants or bank clerks. Those outside are disguised as shoppers. Hidden all around are unmarked police cars and motorcycles.

One detective acts as 'eyes'. Usually he watches from a high point, such as a window. He radios news of the villain's movements to the other detectives and signals when it's time to spring the traps.

BY MID-MORNING THEY ARRIVE AT THE SWISS BANK...

DON'T BE LONG BILL... JUST GIVE HIM A QUICK WALK AROUND THE BLOCK.

...WHERE THE MANAGER AWAITS THEM IN THE VAULTS.

THIS IS THE REAL PRINCESS!

SUCH ELEGANCE... TRULY, HER BLUE BLOOD SHOWS!

WE HAVE ONLY AN HOUR TO PREPARE. WHEN THE IMPOSTER ARRIVES, PRETEND TO BELIEVE HER STORY. IT'S HER ACCOMPLICE I WANT... WE MUSTN'T SPRING THE TRAP 'TIL WE'VE GOT THEM BOTH!

BUT THE STAKE-OUT PLANS ARE DOOMED. AT THAT VERY MOMENT A CAR WITH TWO FAMILIAR PASSENGERS IS DRAWING UP... AS ALWAYS, THE FLAT MAN IS AT LEAST ONE STEP AHEAD.

IT'S THE SECURITY OFFICER. THE FAKE PRINCESS HAS ARRIVED!

QUICK... THE EMERGENCY STAIRS. WE'LL HAVE TO MANAGE WITHOUT OLD BILL!

THIS WAY, PRINCESS. WE'LL HIDE IN THE FOYER.

I AM OLGA... HEIRESS TO THE WOZINSKY FORTUNE.

DO YOU HAVE PROOF?

OF COURSE... THIS DIAMOND... AND THE OLD FAMILY ALBUM WITH MY FINGERPRINTS.

VERY GOOD! BUT WE MUST COMPARE YOUR FINGER PRINTS WITH THE ALBUM. A MERE FORMALITY.

THE IMPOSTER SEEMS CALM AS EACH OF HER FINGERPRINTS IS CAREFULLY INKED AND ROLLED...

BUT... THESE PRINTS MATCH PERFECTLY!

THE WOZINSKY FORTUNE IS YOURS!

DIAMONDS!

IN THE FOYER...

THIS WAY, PLEASE. MY CHAUFFEUR IS JUST OUTSIDE.

OH NO, IT'S BILL... TROUBLE!

HEY THERE! YOU'RE NOT PRINCESS OLGA! HELP! STOP!

GOT HER!

NO BILL... NO!

SAMANTHA! OH - HOW COULD YOU?

GUARDS... QUICK! THE MAN IN THE DOORWAY... STOP HIM!

DON'T LET HIM ESCAPE. HE'S IN THIS WITH ME.

BUT IT'S TOO LATE...

VROOOO

GRRRRRRRRRR!

ONCE AGAIN, THE FLAT MAN GETS AWAY. VERY SOON HE IS SAFELY AIRBORNE, EN ROUTE TO HIS HIDEAWAY. BUT HE STILL SMARTS FROM HIS LOSS...

AND SO...

PRINCESS OLGA CLAIMS THE WOZINSKY FORTUNE...

AND DEVOTES HERSELF TO REWARDING HER FAITHFUL COMPANION.

WON'T YOU HAVE JUST ONE MORE SAUSAGE DARLING?

PERHAPS I CAN SELL THE STORY!

SAMANTHA JONES, FORMERLY OF THE NEWS TEAM, IS JAILED FOR HER PART IN THE ATTEMPTED FRAUD.

AND D.I. SHAMUS AND D.C. WILLIAM WATSON TAKE UP THEIR DUTIES AGAIN AT FUZZVILLE POLICE H.Q.

WELL GUV, I GUESS IT'S BACK TO THE QUIET LIFE...!

I WONDER...

HMMM...!

AS FOR THE NOTORIOUS WEEDY WEEKY (ALIAS 'THE FLAT MAN')

WHO CAN TELL?

Did you guess?

One of the people who knew most about Olga's claim to the fortune – who had an introduction to Olga and a chance to get hold of photographs to help forge identification papers – was the writer of the magazine story. This, as you may remember, was Samantha Jones.

The opportunity was immediately clear to the Flat Man, who read the story in the news. He contacted Samantha and helped her plan the fraud. Through her friendship with Olga, he learned what he needed to know about Olga's plans and movements.

He helped Samantha steal the diamond and the old family album, so they could take out the page showing Olga's baby fingerprints – and put in a fake page with Samantha's fingerprints. With these they could have claimed the fortune – if they had not been outwitted by D.I. Shamus.

HELPING POLICE

Remember – information is the key to crime-fighting.

Try describing people you see, making quick notes on their main features and what they wear. Learn to recognize different kinds of car and to memorize car numbers quickly. Most importantly, learn how to telephone emergency services, such as the police. If you see a crime or accident, phone the police immediately.

DON'T TAKE RISKS! NEVER TRY TO STOP A CRIMINAL.

Answers

DETECTION

Page 117 – The car-swap took place at the parking garage near the bank.

page 121 – The direction in which the broken glass fell shows that the window was probably broken by a ball thrown in from the garden when the door was closed.

SPYCRAFT

Pages 8-9 – The clue to the Spy Post Office Trail is 'Volkswagen'.

Pages 10-11 – Here is what the Quick Code messages say:

At start – 'Meet girl in red hat at clock tower.'

At clock tower – 'Talk about roses to flower seller at fountain.'

At fountain – 'Ask man at statue for light for cigar.'

At statue – 'Stand near church door till old man arrives.'

At church – 'Wait under tree for lady with white cat.'

At tree – 'Man with arm in sling waits on bridge'.

At bridge – 'Buy a dictionary at the book stall and open at page 10.'

At book stall – 'Master spy was the one you last met.'

Page 12 – The music code message says, 'We leave tonight.' The pig-pen code message says, 'Send new code immediately.' The railfence code says, 'Change the password.'

Page 14 – The message in Code T says, 'Watch out for stranger with black hat.'

Page 18 – The password between the lines is 'cola'.

Pages 20-21 – The first few pictures show that the spy is left-handed. The left-handed man in the last picture is the spy, wearing a disguise.

Additional illustration by Malcolm English.
Cover design by Zoe Wray.
With thanks to Vicky Arrowsmith.